ULTRA FLOATING OBJECT™

(also known as)

Whirling-Helicopter Card™
Card Around the Body™

By Geno Munari & Mark Blais

with special materia
Matthew Munar

HOUDINI'S
MAGIC SHOP

---

www.houdini.com

CONTENTS

INTRODUCTION

Congratulations! You have just purchased one of the best secrets in the world of magic.

Over the years, magicians have used invisible thread to fool thousands of people. Now, you will be able to do the same.

In this booklet, talented magicians Mark Blais, Matthew Munari and I will teach you the proper techniques for performing this miracle and give you many ideas for things you can do with the enclosed materials. With a little brain storming, I'm sure you can come up with many more magical effects.

Also included is Matthew Munari's version of the effect and a bonus section *Invisible Thread Mysteries.*

My son and I are the originators of this version of this marvelous effect. It has been called the Floating Card, Whirling Card, Card Around the Body, Helicopter Card and many other names. It is based on Bob Hummer's Whirling Card, a fantastic effect, but different than what you have just purchased. Beware of imitators! These descriptions and explanations are trademarks of mine.

Remember to practice your tricks until you are sure you will be able to do them perfectly before showing them to anyone. And also remember to keep the method a secret.

Enjoy,

Geno Munari

MATERIALS AND PREPARATION

Inside this package you will find twenty to thirty feet of thread wrapped around a card. This thread contains twenty to thirty individual strands of very fine, almost invisible, fiber. When performing, you will be working with just one of these fibers.

To start, cut off a length about three feet long and tape it to the wall at about the same height as your head. It is now necessary to separate one strand of the very fine thread from the mass of thread. Find an individual end strand and start working it loose from the bottom of the bulk, sliding the bulk of the thread from the line. Some people will find it necessary to use a magnifying glass to find an end, although once it's loose, the rest can be done by feel.

Once you have a single strand worked loose a few inches, place a small piece of scotch tape on the end of the thread and wrap the thread around the tape two or three times.

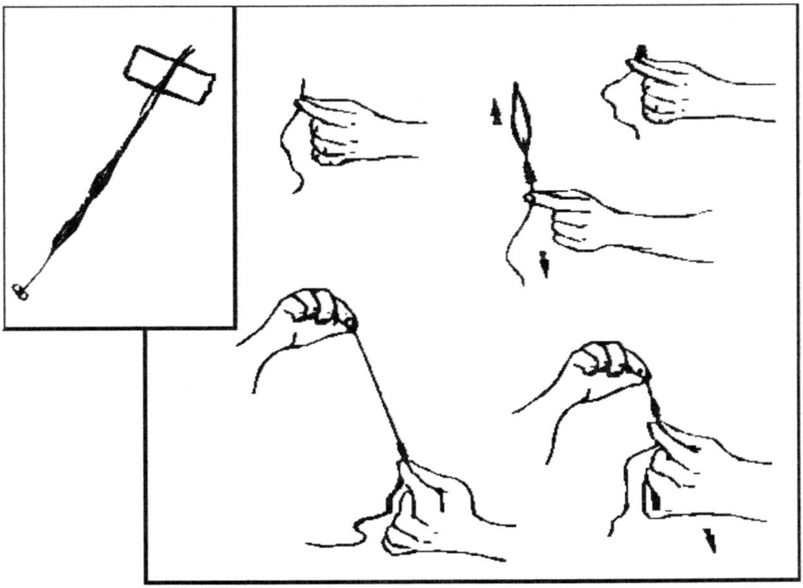

Stick the piece of tape behind your left ear, so now you will have the thread going from behind your ear over to the wall. Continue easing more of the separated strand out. When you feel tension, un-bunch the mass by sliding it up the length of thread, toward the wall. Working two or three inches at a time, until you have a complete single strand of invisible thread a little longer than the length of your arm.

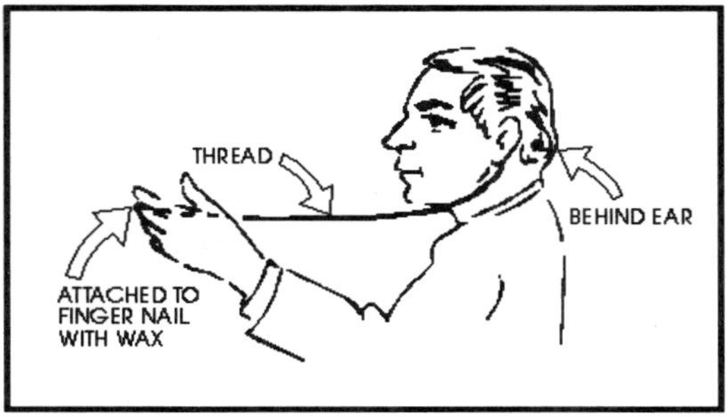

Break the thread at this point and let it hang from your ear. Take a small piece of the wax, roll it into a ball about one-eighth inch in diameter, and hold it in your right hand. With your left forefinger and thumb, take hold of the thread at your ear and run your hand down the thread until your arm is fully extended in front of you. Now stick the ball of wax onto the thread at the left forefinger and thumb, rolling the wax and thread together between your fingers so they become well entangled. If there is any excess thread hanging from the waxball, just break it off.

We should mention that the first time you go through this procedure it will take you a bit of time. But after you've done it a few times, you will be able to get set up in less than a minute.

What you have at this point is a length of invisible thread taped behind your left ear and hanging down below your waist with a small ball of wax at the end. (See illustration) Stick the ball of wax to a button on your shirt, or, if you don't have a button, you can stick it directly to your clothing. This is your basic setup.

To determine the correct length of thread for your specific

size, the end with the ball of wax is placed under the nail of the middle finger of the hand on the same side as the ear attachment. That is, if you prefer to use your right hand for the thread attachment, the other end is attached behind the right ear. If you prefer the left hand, the left ear is used. Your elbow should be against your body and your arm and hand perpendicular to the body as if shaking hands. For the correct length, the thread should be straight with no slack between your finger and ear.

Until you are ready to perform, the end with the ball of magician's wax is attached to one of the buttons on your shirt.

When you are ready to perform a floating trick, in a casual manner so it is not noticed, scrape the wax off your button onto the pad of your right thumb.

To perform with a card, pick up the card with your left hand and as you transfer it to your right hand, place your right thumb onto the center of the card, pressing down and transferring the wax to the card. You will find that if you stick the wax onto the center of the picture card, it is less noticeable.

1. THROWING A CARD FROM HAND TO HAND

Hold a card that is attached to the invisible thread in front of you with one of the long edges toward you. Grip the card at the right hand corner closest to you, with your right middle finger below and thumb on top. Your right forefinger is placed at the right hand corner away from you. (See illustration)

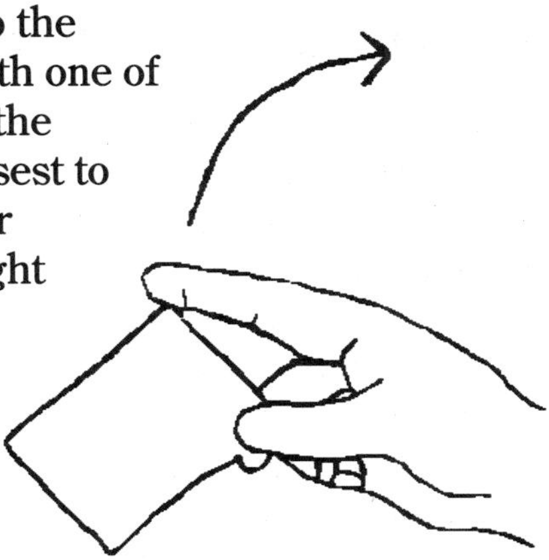

Now bend your right hand at the wrist. When you toss the card, let go with your thumb and middle finger. As the card leaves your hand, it will rotate off your forefinger, causing the card to spin. This should be done with a quick, snapping motion of the wrist. With a little practice, you will be able to spin the card from the right hand to the left hand. Next, practice spinning the card back from your left hand to your right hand.

2. FLOATING A CARD IN MID-AIR

With your left hand, spin the card as described above. As the card begins to arc to the right, catch the thread in the crotch of your right hand, between the thumb and forefinger. The card will appear to be spinning in mid-air directly below your right hand. By placing your left hand palm up under the card, the floating will appear more magical.

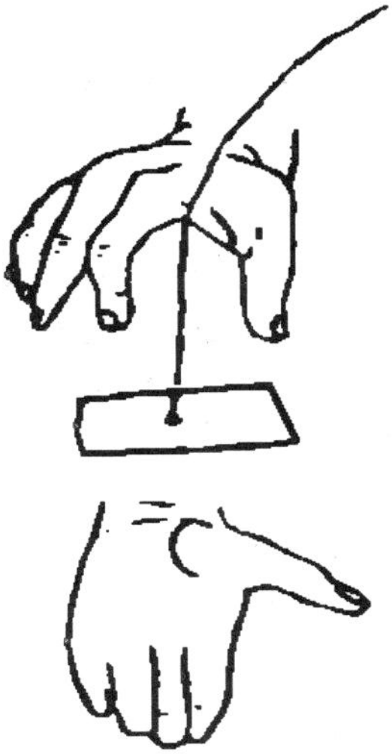

3. LEVITATING A CARD TO YOUR HAND

While floating a card in mid-air, as described above, slowly move your right hand away from your body and the card will float right up to your hand.

4. SPINNING A CARD THROUGH A HOOP

Spin the card with your left hand and catch it in the crotch of your right hand as described in effect #2. Next interlace your fingers together, so the thread and card are hanging between your arms. (See illustration)

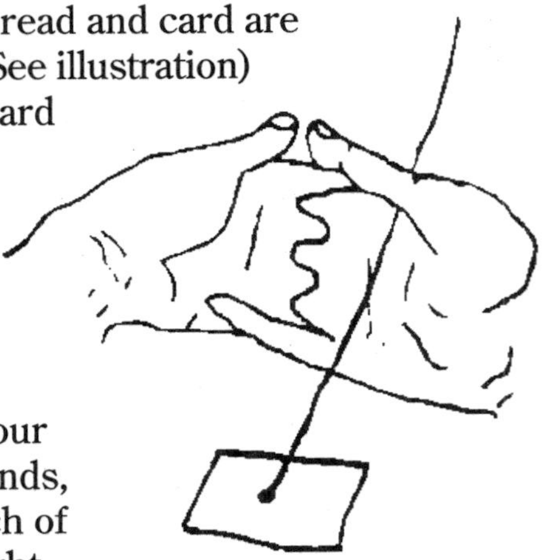

Raise your arms and your card will rise. Once the card has risen to about the height of your left shoulder, lower that shoulder and the card will pass over your left arm. Appearing to have passed through the hoop formed by your arms. Finally, separate your hands, keeping the thread in the crotch of your right hand. Extend the right hand away from you to catch the card.

5. SPINNING A CARD THROUGH A FINGER HOOP

Spin a card from your left hand and catch the thread in the crotch of your right hand. Place the tips of your thumbs and middle fingers together. Let the thread slide to the "V" between your thumbs. (See illustration) Now extend your arms away from your body and the card will rise to just beneath the hoop you've formed with your thumbs and middle fingers.

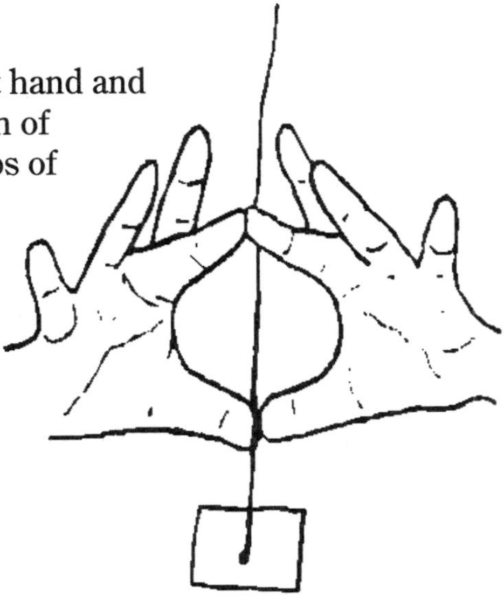

6. SPINNING A CARD THROUGH A HOOP REPEATEDLY

Begin as in the above effect(#4), but instead of interlacing the fingers, just hold your arms close together. As the card passes over the left arm, begin to raise the left shoulder. The thread will hit the back of the left wrist or fingers. When it does, just separate the hands slightly and the thread will go between the hands. This can be repeated as many times as you like.

7. CARD RISING ON HAND

There are two methods:
#1 - Place a card that has the thread attached to it on your left hand with the wax side face up. With the right hand, turn the card over end for end so the wax side is face down and the thread is coming over to the far edge of the card. The edge of the card closest to you should be against the fleshy part of the palm. (See illustration)
By slowly moving your hand forward, the card will rise off your hand and stand straight up. Actually, don't let it get

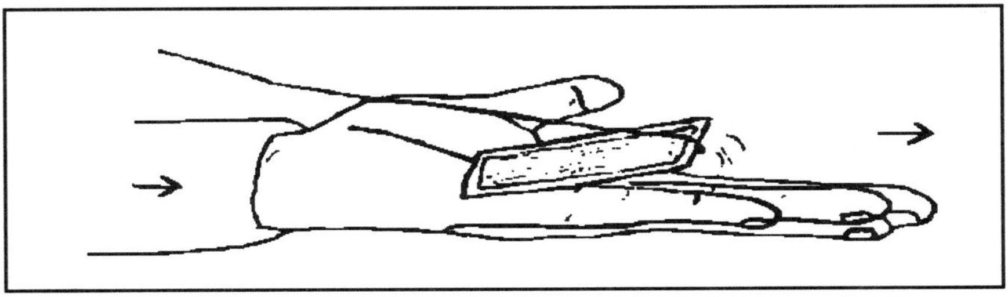

exactly perpendicular or it will fall back toward you.
#2 - Someone can hand you a business card and it will very slowly raise up from one end off of your face up palm. Have the thread affixed to the second finger nail of your left hand and the back of your left ear. Simply have your palm face up, with plenty of slack in the thread. Make sure that the thread lays on your hand in a straight line from the tip of your second

finger to the middle of the back of your palm. Position the card so that it rests longways across your palm and on top of the thread. Slowly extend your arm and take the slack out of the thread. The card very slowly levitates off the palm. One end of the card will rest on the hand. If you place a small bend in the card nearest to the center as possible, the card will balance evenly and completely float up off the palm. Remove the slack and the card will go back to the palm. Immediately hand it back to the spectator.

8. SPINNING A CARD AROUND YOUR BODY

Grip the card in your right hand, making sure the thread runs from your ear across your left cheek, and to your right hand. (See illustration)

Give the card a good, strong spin. As the card begins to arc from right to left, turn your head to the left. With a lot of practice, you will be able to spin the card completely around your body, catching it in the left hand. The thread will now be wrapped around your neck. To unwind it, with the left hand, spin the card back around the body in the opposite direction. Because the thread is shorter due to being wrapped around your neck, the card will have to be spun from a higher position. When it spins back around, catch it in the right hand.

Don't get discouraged attempting this trick. It is the hardest trick in this book and many magicians have a hard time perfecting it.

9. CARD SLIDING ON A TABLE

Place a card on the table with the wax side down and the thread fully extended from your ear. By moving your head back just a little, the card will move on the table. Tell your audience that this is accomplished by your psychic powers.

10. CARD AROUND THE BODY MULTIPLE TIMES

This is a gag to pull on someone who knows how the trick works. Strip out a very long piece of thread (about four feet for a room of average height) and tape it to the ceiling. The thread should hang down to about your waist. Attach a piece of wax to the end of the thread and leave it hanging while you wait for your victim to show up. When ready to perform, move to the area where the thread is hanging, secretly find the wax ball and attach it to a card you have in your hand. If you stand in the right location, you can spin the card and it will rotate around your body several times. This really stumps those who think they know how the trick works.

11. TRICKS WITH OTHER CARDS

The first ten tricks can also be performed with other types of cards, such as a driver's license, credit card, business card, hotel room key card, etc. You will find that with lighter weight cards, like business cards, you will have to give the card a harder spin so it will spin longer but you must be sure when you release the card that there is no slack in the thread, or it will most likely break.

12. RISING CARDS

This effect uses the behind the ear hook up, but the wax is stuck to the left little finger nail. With a little practice, you will find that you can handle a deck of cards as you normally would, even with the thread attached to your little finger.

Start this trick by having two cards selected. While the cards are being looked at by the spectators, hold the cards in your right hand, perpendicular to the floor with the fingers in front and thumb behind. The faces should be toward the spectators. The cards are taken into the left hand in the following manner. The left hand approaches the deck from the top and is passed over the face of the deck until the left little finger is at the bottom left corner of the deck. The thread is now across the top and face of the deck. Support the deck with the little finger at the bottom left, while the three other fingers take the deck on the left side and the thumb takes it on the right side. Once you are holding the deck in this manner, remove the right hand.

Take one of the selected cards from a spectator and place it into the deck so that it will push the thread down into the deck. (See illustration) You will find that you have to move the deck toward yourself to get some slack in the thread and to prevent it from breaking. Also, place this first card about in the middle of the deck.

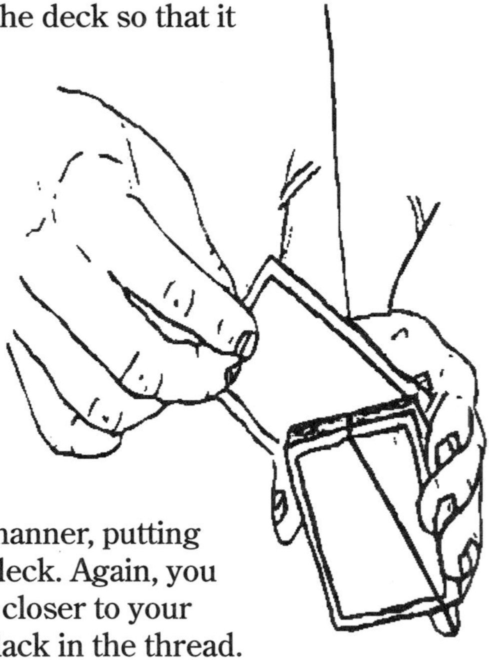

Next, place the second selected card into the deck in the same manner, putting it into the front half of the deck. Again, you will have to move the deck closer to your face to get the necessary slack in the thread. As you do this, blow on the deck, explaining that your magical breath will cause the cards to rise out of the deck. This gives you an excuse for having the cards so close to your face.

You will now find that by moving the deck away from you, the first card will rise from the deck. When it is most of the way out, remove it with your right hand. Continue moving the deck forward and the second card will rise. Remove it from the deck. Take the deck in the right hand, moving your left hand away, and you can hand the deck out for inspection.

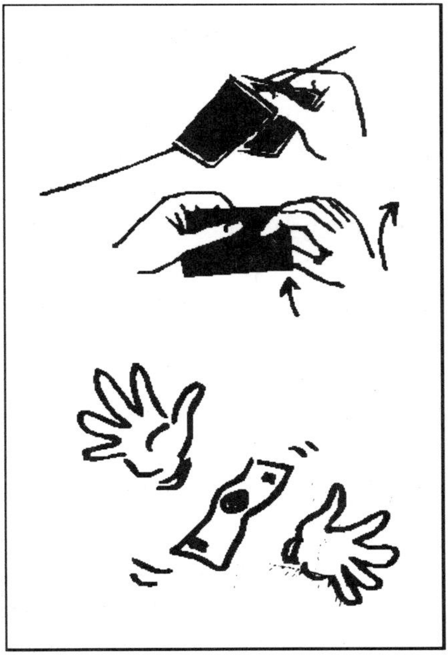

13. FLOATING DOLLAR

Ask for the loan of a bill (try to get one without any tears in it) and place it face up in a spectator's palm, and ask the spectator, "Do you believe in the hereafter?" Before they can answer, grab the bill and say, "Now you know what I am HEREAFTER." This usually gets a laugh. Sneak the wax end from your button onto your nail as you are asking for the bill. Reach for the bill with your right hand and fold it in the middle and place over the thread in sort of a tent fashion.

Then grab the top of the bill (the tent or roof portion of the bill) with the left thumb and fingers. You are squeezing the thread and bill together, and with the right thumb and fingers, twist the bill a quarter of a turn to the right. This will prevent the bill from rolling off the thread. You don't have to twist too tightly, just enough to keep the bill on the thread with enough slack to allow the bill so slide up and down the thread.

Remove the left hand and place it with your right hand on your outstretched left palm. Very slowly extend your arm and the bill will float up off your palm. Position your right and left hand equal distance from the bill to create the illusion of the bill floating above both hands. (Fig. 3) You can slide the bill up and down the thread and animate it by moving the middle finger that has the wax affixed. Finally, you can slide the bill very gently back into the left face-up palm. Carefully open the bill and lift it off the thread. Immediately hand it back to the spectator.

14. FLOATING A SILK HANKY

This effect uses a 6" to 8" silk hanky. A small plastic hoop (4" diameter or larger) can also be used to increase the mystery. When ready to perform, take out the hanky and hoop and hand them to a spectator for examination. While the items are being inspected, remove the wax from the button and attach it to your right middle finger pad or under the nail.

Take back the hanky with the left hand and, by feel, because you won't be able to see the thread, drape the hanky over the thread. Using both hands, tie a loose knot in the hanky around the thread. Move your right hand toward your body somewhat and you will be able to set the hanky on your left palm. Now, by moving your hand up and down and back and forth from your body, the hanky floats around in front of you.

To make the hanky pass through the hoop, hold the hoop horizontal to the floor in the left hand, then let the hanky drop down through the hoop and then back up by moving your right hand. To finish, let the hanky float back down to your left hand, untie it, and hand it to a spectator for examination.

15. FLOATING OTHER SMALL OBJECTS

Using the technique described in #13, (Floating Dollar), you can float any small object, such as a coin, matchbook, bottle cap, drinking straw, etc. Other suggestions include:

Balloon, Business Card, Catsup or Mustard packet, Cigarette, Cocktail stir stick, Comb, Cork, Corn or Potato chip, Crumpled paper, Feather, Flower, Key, Key chain, Leaf Matches, Miniature umbrella, Move a coin, Paper clip, Penny shell on dime, Pickle, Popcorn, Ring rope, Rubber band, Spoon, Stick of gum, Straw, String, Sugar or Equal pack, Sunglasses, Tissue. .and many others!

Pencil Thru Glass

A pencil is pushed thru two cards and a sheet of plastic. The cards removed have a hole thru them but the plastic is unharmed!

$9.95

Mystic Papers

Objects can vanish, change then re-appear!

$3.95

Zig Zag Card

A whole card magically divides into three parts, then it restores itself back to a whole card and can be taken out of frame and examined!

$9.95

Snapper

Snapper will snap for you, but not for anyone else! Under your control always!

$2.95

Trick Deck

The secret deck of magicians and card sharps! Find the selected card instantly! Pull all four aces from the deck! There are hundreds of tricks possible with this deck!

$4.95

Hot Rod

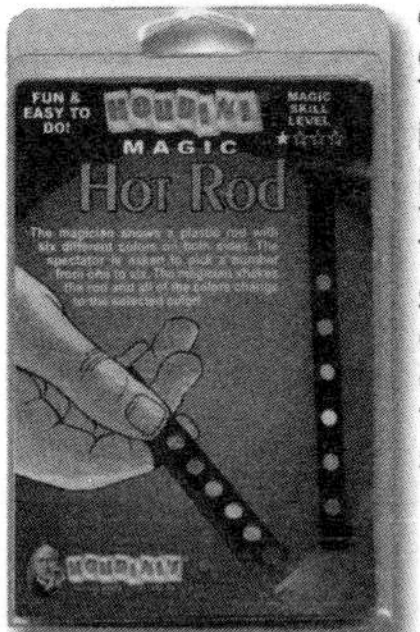

The magician shows a plastic rod with six different colors on both sides. The spectator is asked to pick a number from one to six. The magician shakes the rod and all of the colors change to the selected color!

$4.95

Houdini Chain Escape

A spectator chains you up securely but you escape without difficulty!

$6.95

Color Vision Box

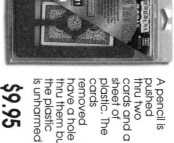

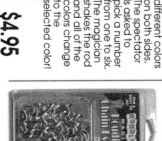

While out of sight of the magician, a spectator places a tube into a covered box. The magician announces that they can read the spectator's mind and accurately names the selected color. This trick can be repeated.

$4.95

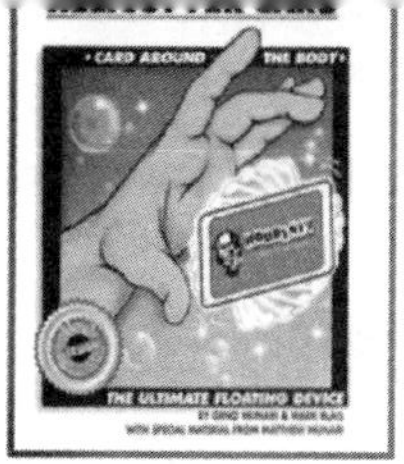

midair, flown all the way around the body with no visible means of support. The object is then handed back to the spectator. This package includes a book with complete instructions.

$19.95

card. Magically, the card rises out of the deck. It can also raise more than one card. Includes book of 20 tricks. Available in Regular or Jumbo.

$24.95 regular
$39.95 jumbo

Slydini Encores on CD
$12.95

The Jinx on CD
$19.95

The Phoenix on CD
$19.95

D'Lite Everyone This Season

Show your hands empty then, magically, your fingertips glow! Pass the glow from hand to hand or even through solid objects. Rocco's D'lite is simple to use and available in both adult and junior sizes. D'lite always attracts a lot attention and provides countless hours of fun!

$29.95

Get Your Favorite Gags

Instantly transform some ones beverage into a totally non-edible sludge!

$1.95

No bartender should be without the classic bug in the ice cube gag!

$1.95

Put a dollar on the ground and when they go to pick it up, snatch it away!

$3.95

We have over a hundred gags & pranks to choose from!

Send orders to: 6455 Dean Martin Dr., Ste. L, Las Vegas, NV 89118
or Call: 702-798-4789 Toll Free: 877-DINI-WHO Fax: 702-798-0045
or ORDER ONLINE AT: WWW.HOUDINI.COM

Check out the backside for other magic must-haves

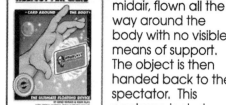

with book of instructions

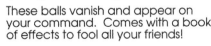

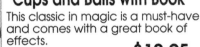

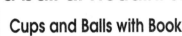

5"
8"
10"

5" $16.95

8" $29.95

10" $49.95

starting at **$4.95** each

Additional Titles:

101 Thumb Tip Tricks
Chinese Linking Ring Book
30 Tips & Tricks with Dime & Penny
50 Tricks with Hot Rod Book
35 Tricks with a Locked Deck
Easy Balloon Animals
Coin Tricks Made Easy
100 Greatest Tricks
Steel Ball & Tube Book
Hooked Coin Book
Ball & Vase Magic
Colorful Magic with the Coloring Book
Slush Powder Book
Folding Coin Book
Magic Wand Book
30 Tricks with Nickels to Dimes
25 Tricks, Tips & Jokes with D'Lite
Inside Secrets of Blackjack
64 Winning Betchas
30 Tips and Tricks with Cups & Balls
The Wax Book
...and many more

We're havin' a ball at Houdini's!

Cups and Balls with Book

This classic in magic is a must-have and comes with a great book of effects.

$10.95

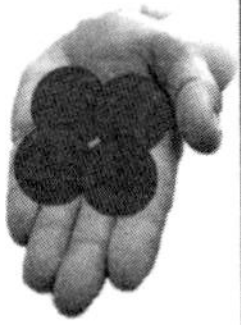

Sponge Ball Magic with Book

These balls vanish and appear on your command. Comes with a book of effects to fool all your friends!

$10.95

$ Magic with Money $

Scotch and Soda with book

Includes book with 55 tricks! A copper and silver coin are placed in a spectator's open palm. The magician pushes the silver over the copper coin and the copper coin passes right through the spectators hand!

$29.95

Lethal Tender with book

The worlds fastest coin trick! A brass and a silver coin, shown in a wallet, can change places with the touch of a card! Easy yet powerful coin magic! Comes complete with a book of 23 tricks!

$39.95

Send orders to: 6455 Dean Martin Dr, Ste L, Las Vegas, NV 89118 or Call: 702-798-4789 Toll Free: 877-DINI-WHO
ORDER ONLINE AT: WWW.HOUDINI.COM

16. RING CLIMBING A PENCIL

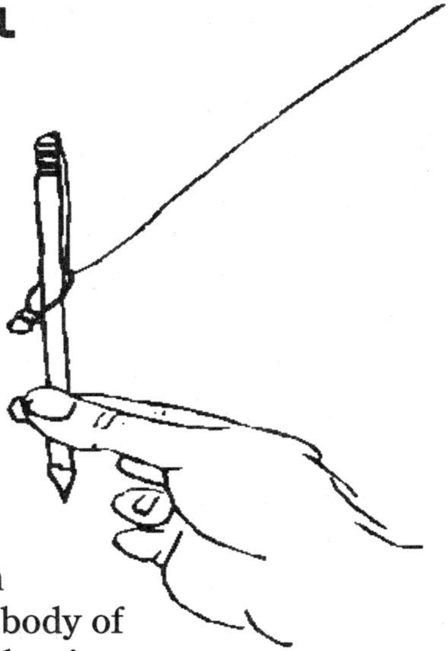

Stick the wax to the eraser end of a pencil and place the pencil in a breast pocket. When ready to perform, borrow a finger ring and remove the pencil from your pocket. Hold the pencil vertically with the eraser end up and the thread hanging loosely down the side of the pencil. Now, drop the ring on the pencil.

By moving the pencil away from you, the ring will slowly rise up the body of the pencil. (See illustration) When the ring gets near the top, remove it and hand it back to the spectator.

17. MOVING OBJECTS UNDER A GLASS

By sticking the wax on the end of the thread to a small object to move inside the glass. Although this can work on a table with a tablecloth, it works easier and better on a smooth table.

18. FLOATING OBJECTS IN A CORKED BOTTLE

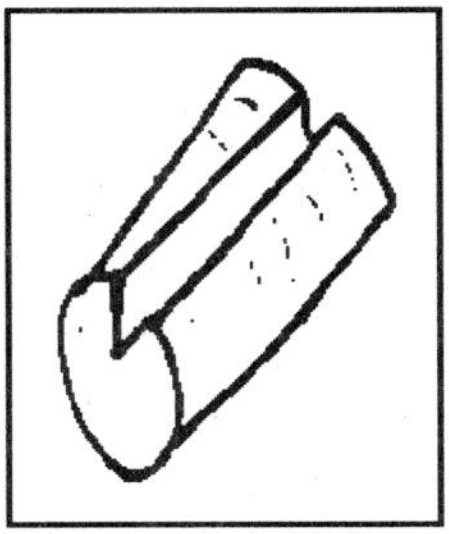

You need to be a few feet away from your audience to perform this trick effectively.

To prepare, find a clear glass wine bottle and soak off the the labels. You will also need a cork from the wine bottle. Prepare it by cutting a notch in it. (See illustration)

Obviously, the objects which can be floated inside the bottle have to fit through the opening. A dime will fit, as will a cigarette. Or just crumple a piece of paper that would be about the diameter of a dime.

If using a piece of paper, start by showing a 4" by 4" square. The invisible thread wax is on the pad of your right thumb. As you start to crumple the paper, stick the wax to it. Once you have a small ball, drop it into the bottle so it falls to the bottom.

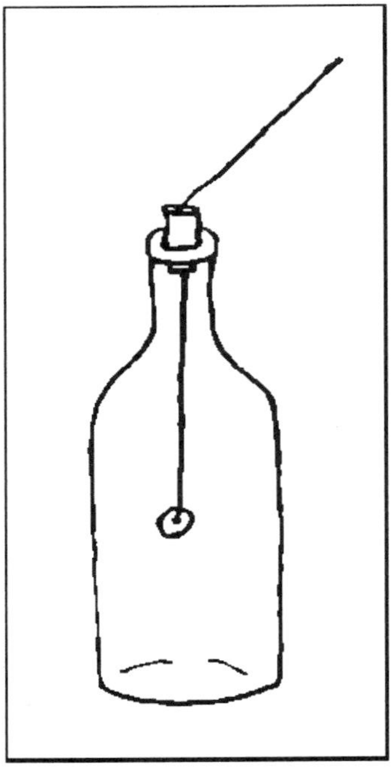

Pick up the cork with your left hand, keeping the notch part toward you. As you start to put the cork in the bottle, guide the thread into the notch with your right hand. The paper can be made to rise inside the bottle in two ways. You can pick up the bottle and move it forward, or better yet, the ball of paper can rise without you touching the bottle by slowly backing away from it.

19. TELEKINESIS

Place a tubular object (like a cigarette or pencil) on a smooth surfaced table.

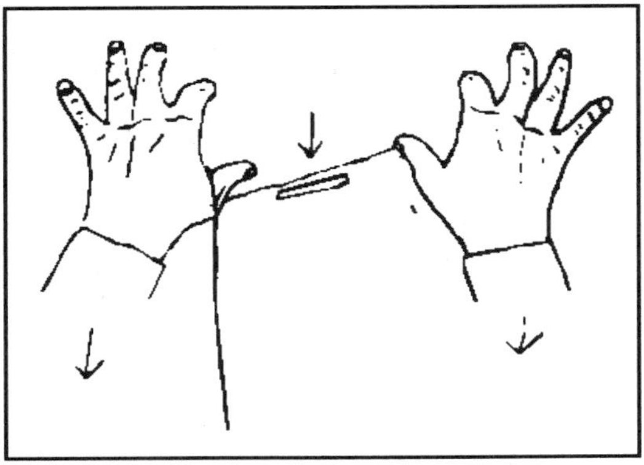

Begin by moving your hands back and forth near the sides of the object, without touching it. On the third or fourth pass, as your hands are moving away from you, blow on the object without pursing your lips, so it is not apparent you are blowing. The object will roll away from you.

Repeat this a second time, making it obvious that you are

blowing. Your audience now thinks they know how it is done. Say that you will make it roll toward you, something that blowing can't accomplish.

You should be set up with the thread and wax attached to your right thumb pad. Catch the middle of the thread in the crotch of your left hand and move your hands to the sides of the object so the thread runs parallel to the object. Start moving your hands back and forth as before. On the third or fourth pass, as your hands are moving toward you, lower them so the thread hits the object and causes it to roll back toward you.

20. CAUSING OBJECTS TO FALL

With the thread attached to the back of the right thumbnail, stand a small object (like a cigarette or lighter) on the table. Begin by circling the object with your right forefinger, keeping your thumb back so the thread doesn't touch the object. (See illustration) Make it obvious that you are not touching the object.

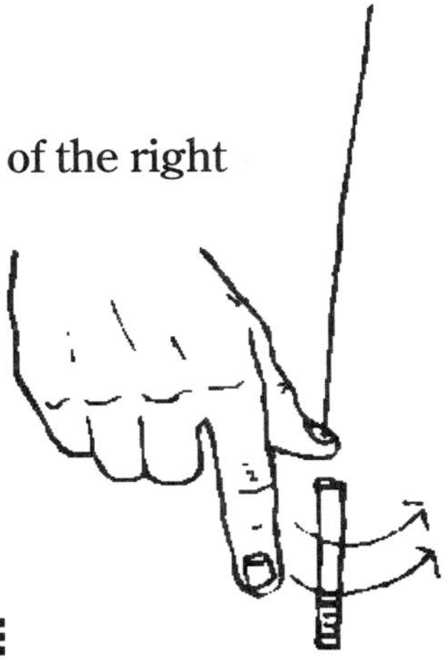

21. STANDING A CARD ON EDGE

For this trick, the thread is not attached behind your ear. You will use a length of thread with wax attached to both ends. Stick one end of the thread to the underside of the table opposite to where you are and run the thread across the table and over the edge, attaching a small coin to the hanging end. If there is a heavy object on the table, such as an ashtray, the far end of the thread can be attached to it, rather than on the underside.

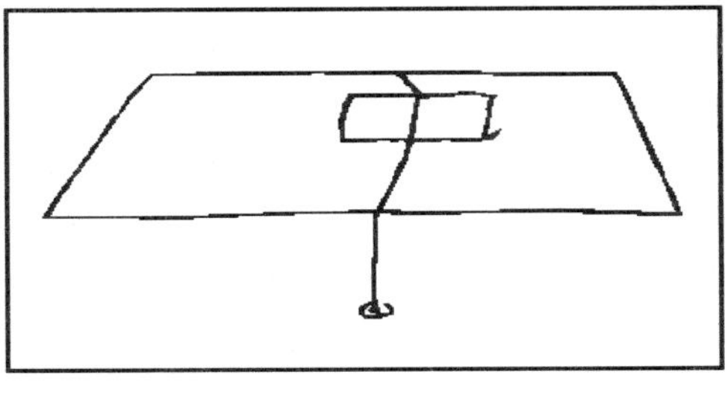

22. FLOATING PEN

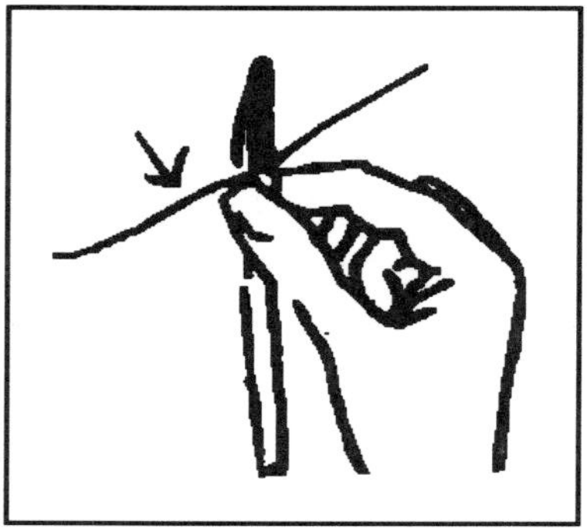

It is amazing how strong the ultra fine thread is. It will even support the weight of a ball point pen. The best type to use are the BIC barrel-style pens. The cap can be used as a guide to place the pen on the thread. The cap should be on the pen concealing the point. The wax on the tip of your outstretched hand, on your second finger. Pick up the pen with your right hand and at the same time remove the slack in the thread until you feel a slight pulling on your left ear. The cap of the pen with the extended clip should be facing the thread.

Approach the thread at the middle of the barrel, just below the cap. Very easily let the clip slide over the thread until it stops. Very gently release the pen from your right fingers and the pen will float. The balance of the pen will give special action to the pen's movement, resulting in a "miracle". With a little practice you could actually be writing with the pen and levitate it out of your hand and off the paper.

THE MATTHEW MUNARI FLOATING CARD ROUTINE

What you are about to read might give you the knowledge to impress friends, meet women (or men), and win a bar bet from an unsuspecting friend.

Imagine if you will... you are with someone.. .you ask to borrow their driver's license, business card, dollar bill, etc... you take the object without any suspicious moves, give it a spin and the borrowed object levitates between two outstretched hands! That means the fingers are separated exactly in the middle of two fixed objects.. .no visible means of support.. .alien technology! Prepare to qualify...

You are supplied with two very important tools - the invisible thread and magician's wax. Do not underestimate the power of an invisible string. It will take the harshest critic and reprogram his brain!

STEP 1: Unwind three feet of the thick cable supplied with the trick. Cut it off, and tape it to a wall or another fixed object. Go to the very end of the thread (the freely hanging section), and pinch one strand of thread with your thumb and fingernail. Tighten the slack up by gently pulling on it. When you have a few inches separated, attach a small ball of wax to the end of the thread.

STATUS CHECK - You should now have a single strand of thread separated from the three foot piece taped on the wall. At the bottom end of the thread, you should have a small ball of wax rolled up. (No larger than the size of a small mole)

STEP 2: Push the rest of the thread up, so the single strand is now approximately two feet long, and take a piece of scotch tape (about the size of your thumbnail) and tape it to the top of the thread, breaking it near the top.

STATUS CHECK - A single strand of thread with tape on one end, and wax on the other. If you get confused at any point during this lesson, refer to this: a string with tape on the top, wax on the bottom that is it!

STEP 3: Put the tape behind your left ear.. .yes, behind your left ear. This is a technique I credit to John Haar, who was famous for his walk-a-way floating bill. With the tape behind your ear, put the wax under your left thumbnail. (If you are left handed, reverse this) Stretch out your left hand and see how far the thread will extend. If you cannot extend your left hand completely, the thread is too short and you will need a new piece. If there is considerable slack in the thread, then you need to shorten the thread by rolling the ball of wax into itself, thereby shortening the wire until it is completely tense when you extend your hand.

"THE THUMBNAIL IS THE KEY"

When you have an arm's length of thread with perfect tension between the thumb and the ear when the thread is stretched out, you are ready to perform the trick. Any thing you touch will levitate... Start by picking up a playing card with the left hand. ..try to apply the wax from underneath the thumbnail to the object one handed. If you need to use two hands at first that's okay, but to get the full effect it must look as if nothing out of the usual has happened, just the natural handling of the card. Aim for the center of the card, that is the center of gravity.

STATUS CHECK - The wax is now supporting the card from falling onto the ground, anchored by the ear. It floats by itself if you lean forward just a tad. This is the start of something big...

STEP 4: Extend the left hand and catch the thread between the webbing of the first finger and thumb. This is the part of the trick that will separate your body and the object. If you did not use your left hand as a lever, the card would try to align itself with your ear, thereby hitting your body and dangling like a puppet on a string. Let the card hang between your thumb and first finger, spreading them as much as possible, and let your right hand take the card like a frisbee.

STEP 5: Spin the card very slowly at first, stabilizing its lateral movement. You need to get the"tight spin" before you throw it around your body. Practice this dutifully and your patience will reward you. As with anything beyond the title of "mediocre", this takes time. Some of you will master this within a matter of seconds, while other may take weeks to perfect it. Whatever the case, don't give up.

If the card is bouncing around wildly on the thread, or is flying 20 feet away, try extending the thread until you feel a slight tug on your ear, then spin it. All slack must be removed from the thread. When you have the spinning down, place the decoy hand (right hand) underneath the spinning object.. .it will appear as if a card is levitating between your hands. Practice this until you feel you cannot be "figured out" by your closest friends. You will discover it is better to mess a trick up in front of your friends than in front of a complete stranger. You now have the power to float things!

The card is unique because you can spin it, and with a little practice you can spin a card like the Aussies spin a boomerang. Not only can you apply the wax to the center of a card, you can use matchbooks, dollar bills or.. .use your imagination! Animate the object you are floating by moving the fingers on the left hand. Wiggle the fingers of the left hand to divert attention to the right hand. The possibilities are limitless. The audience won't believe you are using any type of strings!

"AROUND THE BODY"

This is the ultimate! I don't care.. .I have shown this to a million magicians, and even though I can break my hands showing the most hard core sleight of hand, this is the trick they want to see. When a magician is fooled, the public is floored. Win a drink from a friend, amaze an audience of skeptics, be the hit of the party. (But be prepared to pay the price; you will be asked to perform the trick again, and again).

With the right hand, draw the card to the right side of the body and spin it towards your left ear. You should spin with enough velocity to propel around your neck. Catch it with your left hand, then spin it once more around your body to the left side (with your right hand) and catch it with your left hand.

Use your left thumbnail to disengage the wax from the card.

Hand the card to the spectator with the same hand (the left hand) to examine. With a little practice this will become routine. Without flaw you will be able to apply this technique not only to playing cards, but also business cards, credit cards, and many other objects.

When I invented this, I was a novice. I had no idea what I had stumbled onto. Magicians three times my age (I am 24 at the time of this writing) were amazed, asking me how they had never seen this effect.

Let me give you a little background on this trick. Sometime in the 1950's or 60's a man by the name of Bob Hummer had created an effect known as the "Whirling Card". To present this effect you had to wear a top hat and appropriate jacket. It was formal, and could be performed with appropriate chivalry. Not to mean disrespect; on the contrary, the trick fooled other magicians during its time. On the other hand, I discovered the floating card almost by accident. I was a novice magician, throwing cards around a magic shop. Then I discovered that you could attach the wax to the card one handed and spin it. Julie Detmer and Joey Burton also contributed to the trick, adding their own personal subtleties.

BONUS SECTION

INVISIBLE MYSTERIES

by Dondrake

Over the years, the use of invisible thread (IT as magician's prefer to call it), has developed into several different types of thread and many ways to use this wonderful tool. The tricks that I have devised in this publication come strictly from my own imagination and any similarities to other IT effects is purely coincidental. As you read these pages you will be struck by the simplicity of the use of IT. Therefore I encourage you to make up your own tricks with IT.

Invisible thread, as we all know, comes in two distinct and recognizable forms. First we have the normal, non-elastic variety, normally found in a black color, and composed of nylon. This is probably the most common form of IT in use today. Most of the tricks in this book will use the ordinary IT usually sold in bulk from your magic dealer. Once you have purchased your thread in bulk, we will discuss ways of using it.

The next thing you have to do is to separate a single thread from the bulk thread cable. To do this, simply cut the cable the desired length (about 30" in most cases) and separate out a single thread. Once you have this process completed you may proceed to anchor the thread.

There are several different ways to anchor IT. My favorite

way is to use a piece of scotch tape and anchor one end to my collar, while placing a piece of magician's wax on the other end of the IT and then keeping it handy. If you stick the wax end to the middle finger of your hand, you create a sort of "slide" that will enable you to cause a light object to slide back and forth on the thread.

Note: This effect is a Geno Munari original effect and is copyrighted by Geno, a truly great inventor. By tying a silk loosely around the thread, you can cause it to move toward you or away from you, simply by raising or lowering your arm. This method I will call a portable anchor, abbreviated PA in the text.

Another way to anchor is to make the strand of thread about 45" instead of 30" and looping one end around your neck, thus forming one end of the anchor. Another way is to hold one end of the thread in your mouth (attached to a suitable object) while the thread is anchored to a solid object, such as a cup or glass sitting upon a table. Michael Ammar invented this way of using the thread. This method is called a permanent anchor, which I will abbreviate PMT in this text. The only advantage of this method is that it allows you to keep both hands free.

The following tricks are effects that you can do with IT, and each is marked with its appropriate anchor. If any of the following tricks will work with both methods of anchoring, then I will leave it up to the discretion of the magician to decide which one to use. I will not then put any designation in front of the effect! So set up your IT and enjoy! Remember, practice makes perfect so practice at least one hour a day.

TRICKS WITH I.T.

1. THE FLOATING MATCH BOOK (PA)

Produce a book of matches and light someones' cigarette or just light a match. As you close the book of matches, it "floats" in mid air! Now the matchbook floats toward your body and into your shirt pocket. This method is easy. After you open the matchbook, loop it over the IT and close the cover. The opening in the top of the matches will allow it to slide toward your body as you raise your arm. NOTE: It may need a little help from your other hand to actually go into your pocket.

2. THE FLOATING PEN (PA)

As in the above effect, a light weight ball point pen may be floated toward and away from your body, simply by hanging the pen on the thread by using the clip. Be careful when removing the pen, so as not to break the IT.

3. THE FLOATING BILL (PA)

Borrow a bill of any denomination from a spectator and fold it in half. As you fold the bill, make sure you fold it over the thread. Now pretend to "magnetize" the bill by rubbing it on someone's hand. (Thanks to Matthew Munari for letting me include this trick). Now you can cause the bill to float and to slide toward and away from your body! Don't forget to return the bill!

4. NACHO LIGHTS (PA)

When you go into a Mexican restaurant and order nachos, some of the nachos will be curved at the top. This allows you to hand one of the nacho chips on the IT and allow it to "float", and slide back and forth.

5. THE FLOATING FINGER RING (PA)

Using the appropriate finger, make sure the wax end of the IT is attached to that finger nail. Now slide the ring off the finger and onto the thread. The ring will float and slide back and forth as above. Please be careful when detaching the ring from the thread. Allow the ring to slide toward and onto the correct finger. This is a killer trick! (Thanks to Keith Raleigh for inventing this little miracle).

6. THE FLOATING STRAW

I don't know who first came up with this one, but it's a lot of fun at parties. Bend the top of a drinking straw over, so that it forms a hook. Now you can hook it over the thread and make it slide back and forth or, by hooking your opposite thumb under the thread you can make it float up and down.

7. THE FLOATING SILK

Purchase a small silk handkerchief from your magic dealer. Tie the handkerchief in a loose knot a around the thread and then make it do acrobatics in mid air. Then until the silk and pass it around for examination.

8. THE FLOATING COMB

If it is hooked near the end, a pocket comb makes an ideal floating device. Do not hook it too near the center or it will have the tendency to fall off the thread!

9. THE FLOATING CHECK (CPA)

Often when you are writing a check out to pay at the grocery store or elsewhere, it is fun to float the check over to your payee. This gets a good laugh and it is a real attention getter for business!

10. THE FLOATING BUSINESS CARD (PA)

For this one, stick the end of the wax to the card, and hook your thumb under the thread so the card will float up and down. As you move your hand away from your body, the card will apparently float right up to it. As you retrieve the card, use your nail to scrape off the wax before you hand it out! This is a great way to hand out your card!

11. SPIRIT KLEENEX (PMT)

Remove a tissue from a box of tissues and explain to your audience that you have been in touch with the spirits. (To get a good laugh here, remove a bottle of whiskey from your coat pocket and pretend to take a drink). Fold the tissue around your IT and then back away from the anchor, causing the tissue to float up and down as you move towards and away from the anchor. Both hands are now free to pass over the tissue while it is floating. Have the tissue float down to your outstretched hand, and pass it around for examination.

12. THE FLOATING PAPER CLIP

If you work in an office building, this one will drive your co-workers crazy! Simply hook the paper clip over the IT and proceed to float it. Be careful when removing the clip. It is sometimes better to break the thread and hand the clip out for examination, if someone gets too curious!

13. FLOATING A LOAN (PA)

If a friend asks you for a loan of a dollar or five dollars, simply "float" the loan to him, saying, "I hope you can do the same when you pay me back". You may never see the money again, but think of the fun you'll have.

14. FLOATING POPCORN (PA)

When sitting in a movie theater eating popcorn, it's fun to hook it over the thread and float it to you mouth. (You can do so by raising your arms). People sitting around you will think you're a little weird, but think of the advertising!

15. FLOATING FISHING TACKLE (PA)

When you're out fishing with friends, sitting in a boat or on a dock, it's fun to float the lures around before attaching them to your line. The hook on the lures makes it easy to drape them over the thread.

16. STRINGING THEM ALONG (PA)

This is similar to the Floating Ring trick. Keep a piece of string tied around your finger. When your friends ask what it's for, say you forgot. Now allow the loop of string to float back onto your finger. Say, "Now I remember, it was so I wouldn't forget to get airline tickets!"

17. THE FLOATING PLAYING CARD (PA)

If you're sitting at a card table, playing cards with your friend, this is a hot one. When drawing a card (as in Rummy), simply stick the wax to the card and allow it to float up to your hand. You can do this by hooking your thumb under the thread and extending your arm out away from your body! Be sure to remove the wax if your friends want to see the cards.

18. FLOATING MASCARA (PA)

Here's one for the ladies. When you're in the powder room fixing your makeup, simply stick the wax to your eyebrow pencil or lipstick! The other girls will faint when it floats up to your face! This is a good attention getter and allows you to hand out your business card!

19. FLOATING CELLOPHANE

Remove the cellophane from a package of cigarettes and float it in the air. This one can be done by either of two anchors. After floating the cellophane, pass it out for examination!

20. THE FLOATING RUBBER BANDS

You can do your favorite rubber band penetration trick, and then tie the two bands together. They will drape nicely over the thread and float wherever you wish!

21. HEAVIER THAN AIR

Here's a bright idea with a helium balloon. By attaching a small hook to a helium balloon, you can hook the balloon on to the IT. Now it appears that you can make the balloon heavier than air by causing it not to rise. You can unhook it, hand it to a spectator and it will not pull upward. By controlling the thread, you can get some pretty sppctacular effects!

22. THE FLOATING BALL

For this one you will need a silk and a Christmas ornament. Hang the ornament on the thread at the same time as you put a silk in front of it. Now do a small Zombie routine by maneuvering the silk so that it looks like the ball is floating under the silk. Now take the silk away, and the ball still floats! This one is a killer effect and should get you thunderous applause!

23. A LIGHT PAIR OF SHADES

Most plastic sunglasses are easily floatable. Just hook them over the thread and proceed to have them hang in mid air. This looks really good if you happen to have been wearing them first, and replace them on your face after floating them.

24. THE RISING CARD

You can create a spectacular rising card effect by simply sticking a little magician's wax onto the top edge of a previously selected card. As you bring the deck within range of the anchored thread, have the selected card on top of the deck. As you hold the deck in front of the IT, press the wax against the suspended thread and slowly lower the deck. It will appear that the card is rising out of the deck! For a fantastic finish, take the deck away, leaving the selected card hanging in mid air!

100 THINGS TO DO IN TAMPA BAY BEFORE YOU DIE

2nd Edition

KRISTEN HARE

REEDY PRESS

Reedy Press
PO Box 5131
St. Louis, MO 63139, USA
www.reedypress.com

Library of Congress Control Number: 2018945632

ISBN: 9781681061641

Design by Jill Halpin

Printed in the United States of America
18 19 20 21 22   5 4 3 2 1

Photo credits: Kristen Hare

CONTENTS

Music and Entertainment

Sports and Recreation

Culture and History

PREFACE

In 2012, my family moved to Tampa Bay from Missouri for what was supposed to be one year.

It didn't take long to realize we weren't leaving Florida. Writing the first edition of *100 Things to Do in Tampa Bay Before You Die* only made that clearer. We loved being so close to beaches with clear, gentle water and powder sand. We delighted in the wild things everywhere—the lizards, the birds, the sea creatures and, yes, with great caution, the alligators. Maybe most importantly, we felt constantly welcomed by Floridians.

All those things are still true.

But a theme that started after this book came out inspired the more than twenty-five new adventures in this second edition. It is, simply, "don't let the tourists have all the fun."

If you are a tourist, welcome. Here you'll find locals and people from all over the world who take both beach time and hurricane season seriously. We have palm trees and Spanish moss, thriving communities of all shapes and forms, and more local beer than the locals can drink. (Well, most of them.)

And if you're a local, used to the routes you drive and the places you favor, consider this book an invitation to become a hometown tourist. Go to the places you've always wondered about—the festivals, the tours, the classics, and the latest things that you think are just for Florida's visitors.

They're not. They're ours. It's time to get out, explore, discover, savor, and remember, don't let the tourists have all the fun.

Happy travels,
Kristen Hare

ACKNOWLEDGMENTS

For Jai, Max and Leela, who know there's always more to see, do and love in Florida, and to the friends, neighbors, co-workers, acquaintances and strangers who've shared their favorite things to do in Tampa Bay generously and willingly with me in the past six years.

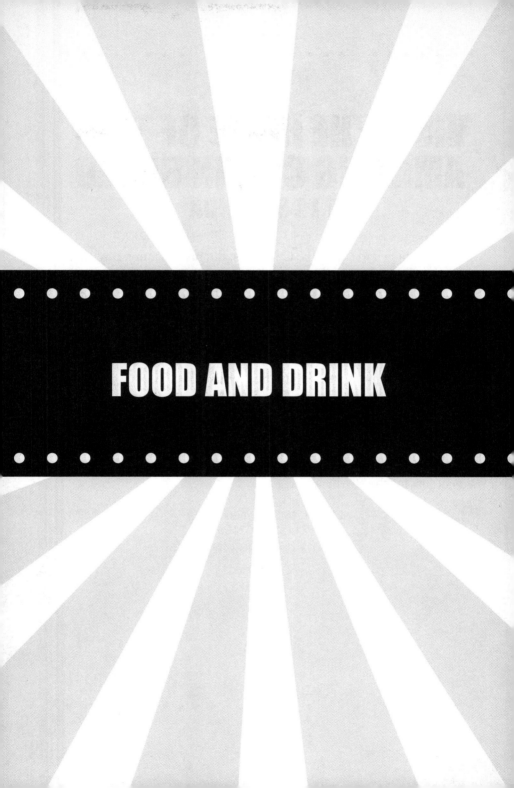

FOOD AND DRINK

1

VISIT THE HOME OF THAT AMAZING CUBAN BREAD

AT LA SEGUNDA

If you've made it to any of the Cuban restaurants in Tampa Bay, then you're familiar with that wonderful, warm, crackly Cuban bread. For a lot of restaurants in the area, including the famous Columbia Restaurant just down the street, that bread comes from La Segunda Central Bakery. This small and easy-to-miss Tampa landmark sits in a quiet spot just a few blocks from Ybor City's popular 7th Avenue. The bakery is more than a hundred years old and outlasted two others that started as parts of a co-op at the same time, La Primera and La Tercera. Inside, you'll find that fresh Cuban bread as well as many other temptations, including the slightly sweeter bread made for Cuban sandwiches, guava turnovers, and a full menu. It's worth a visit just for the smells alone.

2512 N. 15th St., Ybor City
813-248-1531
lasegundabakery.com

2

EAT THAI UNDER THE TREES

AT WAT TAMPA'S SUNDAY MARKET

A golden-roofed Buddhist temple sits along the Palm River, with rows of picnic tables under tall trees dripping with Spanish moss. It's the perfect place for a heaping plate of Thai food each Sunday at Wat Mongkolratanaram of Florida's weekly market. At Wat Tampa, choose from noodle soups, fish and chicken curries, sweet friend plantains and taro, coconut custard, papaya salad, banana leaves with sweet rice inside, and lots, lots more. The market was first established in the late 1980s with just two tables. Now, it's a popular stop for authentic Thai food in a one-of-a-kind setting. The market runs from 8:30 a.m. to 1 p.m. every Sunday. Bring cash—the vendors don't accept cards—and your appetite.

5306 Palm River Rd., Tampa
813-621-1669
wattampainenglish.com

SENILITY PRAYER
Friends are Connected
Heart to Heart
Don't get so busy
making a living
that you
forget to
make a life

3

EAT A BURGER, SIP SOME TEA
AT THE CHATTAWAY

Follow the flower-filled bathtubs into The Chattaway for a really good burger. Outside, you'll find outdoor seating at this dive that first opened in 1951. It's all pink and green and, if you don't notice the Union Jacks everywhere, feels like classic old Florida—plus bathtub planters. Make sure to walk around and see the koi weaving through the water under a covered walkway. Inside, there's no ignoring those Union Jacks, or the tea sets, or numerous images and tributes to England's royal women. A proper English tea is served in the afternoon by Lady Chattaway herself, and if the finger sandwiches, scones, crumpets, and cream aren't filling enough for you, you'll find burgers, cold beer, and quite often live music waiting just outside.

358 22nd Ave. South, St. Petersburg
727-823-1592
thechattaway.com

4

TRY SOME BERRY WINES
AT KEEL AND CURLEY WINERY

Keel and Curley Winery is located in Plant City, the home of the Florida Strawberry Festival and long stretches of strawberry fields. The winery has Sweet Blueberry wine, Strawberry Riesling, Black Raspberry Merlot, and Wildberry Pinot Noir. If berries aren't your favorites, try the crisp and tangy Key Lime Pie, a refreshing white, or the yummy Peach Chardonnay. There's also homemade hard ciders, including Blueberry and Strawberry Lime. The winery offers tastings anytime, and on weekends, come for live music, happy hour, and food trucks. If you're not into the wines, you can also sample beer from Two Henrys, a local brewery with a tasting room at the winery. Try the Blueberry Vanilla Wheat, the Roasted Jalapeño Blueberry Porter, or keep it simple with the 2HB Pale Ale.

5210 Thonotosassa Rd., Plant City
813-752-9100
keelandcurleywinery.com

5

TRY A FAMOUS STRAWBERRY MILKSHAKE

AT PARKESDALE FARM MARKET

The Food Network named Parkesdale Farm Market's strawberry milkshake the "best drinkable dessert." This is accurate. But maybe you'd rather try the strawberry shortcake, or the strawberry jam, or the strawberry cookies. There's even strawberry salad dressing. Whatever you choose, a trip to the old farm stand in Plant City ends with something delicious. The market, which opened in 1956, is open nearly year round except for two weeks in August. As with any good local food, pay attention to the season. If you visit anytime from January to April, get the strawberry shortcake. Any time of the year, grab your treats, a crown, and take a seat in the strawberry throne. Have fun exploring the covered seating area, with pink and green tinsel strawberries dangling everywhere and mementos from the farm's more than sixty-year history, including framed photos of past U.S. presidents who made the same trip, probably for the same good stuff.

3702 W. Baker St., Plant City
813-754-2704
parkesdale.com

6

SEE THE DANCERS
AT COLUMBIA RESTAURANT

There are so many reasons to visit Tampa's famous Columbia Restaurant. The food (including the amazing Cuban bread and famous "1905 Salad"), the drinks (including homemade sangria), the building (you can explore fifteen dining rooms, including the Don Quixote Room and the Red Room), and the ambiance (including all of the above). But there's also the dancing. Every night but Sunday, pay a small cover charge and you'll get to see the swirling skirts and precise poses of the flamenco dancers who are nearly as famous as the restaurant itself. If you can't make it for the nightly shows, don't worry—between the food, the décor, and the history, the Columbia is a show all by itself. If you really like Columbia on East 7th Avenue, the other Tampa Bay locations are also worth a visit and offer great views all their own. Among them, Columbia's location at the Tampa Bay History Center has an al fresco spot on the Riverwalk. In Sarasota, you can people watch while sitting outdoors at St. Armands Circle. And at Clearwater's Columbia location, ask to be seated outside and watch for dolphins.

2117 E. 7th Ave., Tampa
813-248-4961
columbiarestaurant.com

7

GET THE PASSWORD
AT CIRO'S

You won't get in to this hard-to-find spot without a password. You'll get it after making reservations at this 1920s-inspired speakeasy. Next, get directions. Ciro's is tucked into the first floor of an apartment building on Bayshore Boulevard in Tampa, but it's well worth a few passes through the parking lot. Then, knock. Someone will open a window in the door (and no one will blame you for having *Princess Bride* flashbacks). Inside, once your eyes adjust to the dim lighting, pick your drink from a selection that's as much fun to say as it is to drink, including the Rickey and the Gin Daisy. Ciro's has appetizers and a full dinner menu, plus weekday happy hours and late-night weekend happy hours.

2109 Bayshore Blvd., Tampa
813-251-0022
cirostampa.com

8

LOOK FOR THE SNAKES
AT LINGER LODGE

When this restaurant touts that it's "Old Florida," it doesn't mean beaches or quaint, quiet towns. Instead, it's a spot on the balmy Braden River where wildlife still rules, even if only as taxidermy on the walls. Get a reservation, this place fills up fast. And if the weather and the crowds permit, get a seat outside on the covered, screened-in patio and enjoy the water views while you dine. Inside, look for all the wild things, including a giant gator, deer, fish, a jackalope, and some sporty squirrels. Oh yeah, and the snakes. A lot of them. If you aren't sure where to begin, look for the Linger Lodge sign across the room as you walk through the front door. If you've ever wondered how snakes could form letters such as *d* or *g*, there's your answer.

7205 85th St. Ct. East, Bradenton
941-755-2757
lingerlodgeresort.com

9

BIKE OR BUS
TO THE BREWERIES

Tampa Bay has a booming and bountiful local beer scene. Counting breweries that are expected to open soon, the Brewery Bay's helpful directory includes more than a hundred. You're probably wondering how you can ever visit them all. The bad news is they're spread out, and locations such as Leaven Brewing in Riverview or Swan Brewing in Lakeland or Two Henrys Brewing Company in Plant City often require a special trip. But for many of the spots in Tampa and St. Pete, you just need your feet. Use them to pedal with PedalPub St. Petersburg on routes that can take you to several local breweries, including Cage Brewing, 3 Daughters Brewing, Green Bench Brewing Co., St. Pete Brewery, and Cycle Brewing. If all that pedaling's too much for you, try the Brew Bus Tampa Bay or Tampa Bay Brews Cruise, which both have routes that include stops at breweries in St. Pete, Tampa, downtown Tampa, Seminole Heights, Ybor City, and even the breweries that are a bit out of the way. For a look at all the breweries Tampa Bay has to offer, check out thebrewerybay.com.

PedalPub St. Petersburg, 1975 3rd Ave. South, St. Petersburg
727-581-3388, pedalpubstpete.com

The Brew Bus Tampa Bay, 4101 N. Florida Ave., Tampa
877-965-0048, brewbususa.com

Tampa Bay Brews Cruise
813-609-8687, brewscruise.com

PICK YOUR OWN BERRIES
AT WISH FARMS

You'll know it's berry season in Florida when the prices at markets and grocery stores drop. As the growing season ends for most farms, they'll open up and let you skip those stores and pick strawberries and blueberries for yourself. You can visit several in the area, but try Wish Farms, which maintains a list of area farms, for u-pick strawberries and blueberries. Also in Plant City, Keel and Curley's blueberry fields are home to the annual Tampa Bay Blueberry Festival, which includes the chance to pick your own. The festival takes place in April and has free admission. Make sure to get your pie plates and jelly and jam jars ready—you'll probably come home with more than you can possibly eat.

Wish Farms
813-752-5111
wishfarms.com

Keel and Curley Winery
5210 Thonotosassa Rd., Plant City
813-752-9100
keelandcurleywinery.com

11

TACK A DOLLAR TO THE CEILING

AT MAHUFFER'S BAR

Grab a cold drink at this old dive, find a seat, or just wander through the treasure chest of old boat parts, graffiti, and gritty charm at Mahuffer's Bar in Indian Shores. And add a dollar bill to the collection on the ceiling, if you can find room past the bras and dangling lines of old buoys, that is. You can leave those, too. The collage of things is a great reason to stop in for a drink on your way to or on your way home from the beach. Or you could skip the beach completely and get comfortable. But maybe leave a trail of breadcrumbs, or bras, to help you find your way back out again.

19201 Gulf Blvd., Indian Shores
727-596-0226
facebook.com/mahuffers

SHOP FOR ITALIAN FOOD
AT MAZZARO'S

If the sterile, soulless aisles of your average grocery store aren't doing it for you, go to Mazzaro's Italian Market. This St. Pete institution is jam-packed with choices—there's a deli, a cheese room, fresh coffee, handmade pasta, your favorite Italian desserts, freshly made gelato, and lots of people who want exactly the same things. It gets crowded. If you'd rather eat someone else's excellent Italian cooking, check out the full lunch menu, which has soup and savory hot and cold sandwiches. After you order, grab a seat on the covered patio and sit back to people watch. Mazzaro's is open every day but Sunday. If that's your normal grocery shopping day, a visit here just might change that.

2909 22nd Ave. North, St. Petersburg
727-321-2400
mazzarosmarket.com

CATCH
THE FESTIVAL SPIRITS

Tampa Bay has so many festivals in honor of so many adult beverages. You could sip your way, responsibly of course, through the whole year (except for the hottest months, when you're on your own). Here's a sampling:

January

Central Florida Rum and Food Experience, Lakeland
rumandfood.com

February

Beer, Bourbon & Barbecue Festival, Tampa
beerandbourbon.com/florida

Wine Weekend St. Pete, St. Petersburg
wineweekendstpete.org

Punta Gorda Wine and Jazz Festival, Punta Gorda
puntagordachamber.com

March

Hunahpu's Day Release Party, Tampa
cigarcitybrewing.com

Tampa Bay Beer Week, Tampa Bay
tampabaybeerweek.com

Busch Gardens Food & Wine Festival, Tampa
buschgardens.com/tampa

Florida Brewers Guild Craft Brew Festival, Tampa
floridabrewersguild.org

Florida Winefest Auction, Sarasota
floridawinefest.org

April

Tampa Bay Blueberry Festival, Plant City
keelandcurleywinery.com

Best of Tampa Bay, Tampa, strazcenter.org

Los Vinos de Dali, St. Petersburg, thedali.org

Festa Italiana, Ybor City, festaitalianatampa.com
Zoo Brews, Tampa, zootampa.org

May

Tampa Bay Margarita Festival, Tampa
tampamargaritafest.com

Temple Terrace Craft Brew Fest, Temple Terrace
templeterracebrewfest.com

Food and Wine on Pine, Anna Maria Island
foodandwineonpine.com

Clearwater Beach Taste Fest, Clearwater
clearwaterbeachtastefest.com

October

Oktoberfest, Tampa, oktoberfesttampa.com

Oldsmar Oktoberfest, Oldsmar, myoldsmar.com

November

Dunedin Wines the Blues, Dunedin
dunedingov.com

Clearwater Beach Uncorked, Clearwater
clearwaterbeachuncorked.com

Safety Harbor Wine Festival, Safety Harbor
cityofsafetyharbor.com

Dunedin Celtic Music & Craft Beer Festival, Dunedin
dunedincelticmusicfestival.com

Ribfest, St. Petersburg, ribfest.org

14

BET ON THE SUNSET
AT THE SANDBAR ON ANNA MARIA ISLAND

You can choose from a lot of places to eat and drink at the beach around Tampa Bay. At many of them, you can also watch the sunset. At the popular Sandbar Waterfront Restaurant on the postcard-perfect Anna Maria Island, you can even place bets on the setting sun. Every night before the sun sinks into the horizon, servers stop by tables and ask diners to guess the exact time the final slivers of pink and orange will sink into blue. When that happens, a server rings the bell. The winner gets a treat from the more than hundred-year-old island establishment. Everyone else gets dinner at sunset at the beach, toes in the sand or on the deck. Either way, you can't lose.

100 Spring Ave., Anna Maria
941-778-0444, sandbar.groupersandwich.com

TIP

The Sandbar doesn't take reservations, so get there early or grab a drink at the window by the beach and look for shells while you wait.

15

GET THE GROUPER
AT FRENCHY'S IN CLEARWATER

Frenchy's certainly has newer and more colorful locations, but the original spot on Baymont Street in Clearwater is a perfect dive, with wood paneling, a fish tank in the wall, and beer bottle vases. Try the grouper sandwich—grilled, fried, Cajun—however you get it, it's fresh and good. And if you're lucky, you might get to enjoy it while listening to salty locals who are usually tucked in at the bar. If you love the food, check out other Frenchy's locations, including beachfront at Frenchy's Rockaway Grill. If you just love Frenchy's, consider committing to an overnight stay at Frenchy's Oasis Motel. There, you can get that famous grouper sandwich delivered right to you through room service.

41 Baymont St., Clearwater
727-446-3607
frenchysonline.com

16

GET THE DESSERT
AT BERN'S

This famous Tampa strip-mall-turned-steak-palace is the kind of place where it's smart to fast on the day of your reservation (and get reservations early—otherwise, you're not getting in at all). You'll also want to wander around Bern's Steakhouse a bit and take in the red velvet walls of the entrance, the red velvet rail that leads to the restrooms, the gilded portraits, and the dining rooms that each have their own charm—there's one with busts along the walls, and another with a mirror from the original barber shop in that space. And make sure while you're there to visit the room where the dessert happens. The Harry Waugh Dessert Room is on the second floor of the restaurant, and you don't have to stuff yourself with steak and onion rings before you come on up. Settle in to what feels like your own private space made from old wine tanks with blown up images of cookbooks from Bern's collection. Oh, and get something sweet, of course. You'll find pages of desserts, but the real treat is the experience itself.

1208 S. Howard Ave., Tampa
813-251-2421, bernssteakhouse.com

TIP

If you eat at Bern's, ask for the tour. You'll get to see the bustling kitchen and the chilly wine cellar, where bottles of wine are stacked high like books at the library.

17

SAVOR A COFFEE
AT THE OXFORD EXCHANGE

The Oxford Exchange has been many things over the years. In the days of railroad magnate Henry B. Plant, it was the stables for the nearby and once-grand Tampa Bay Hotel. It has also been shops, an insurance office, and a photo studio. Now, with its black-and-white tiled floors and ample sunlight, it's a boutique bookstore that hosts a book club, a treasure-filled shop, and an elegant but simple restaurant serving breakfast, brunch, lunch, and afternoon tea. It's also the perfect place for a coffee or tea break. Start with something from local Buddy Brew coffee. Or you could also have tea. Or a meal. But leave your phone and laptop closed, settle into one of the big couches or hideaway chairs, and soak up this special space.

420 W. Kennedy Blvd., Tampa
813-253-0222
oxfordexchange.com

18

CELEBRATE THE FRUIT
AT A LOCAL FESTIVAL

Fruit is one of our tastiest natural resources, after all, and Tampa Bay has festivals for blueberries, strawberries, oranges, kumquats, and loquats, because of course we do.

January

Kumquat Festival, Dade City
kumquatfestival.org

February

Florida Strawberry Festival, Plant City
flstrawberryfestival.com

Florida Loquat Festival, New Port Richey
ecologyflorida.org

April

Blueberry Festival, Plant City
keelandcurleywinery.com

July

Dunedin Orange Festival, Dunedin
dunedinorangefestival.co

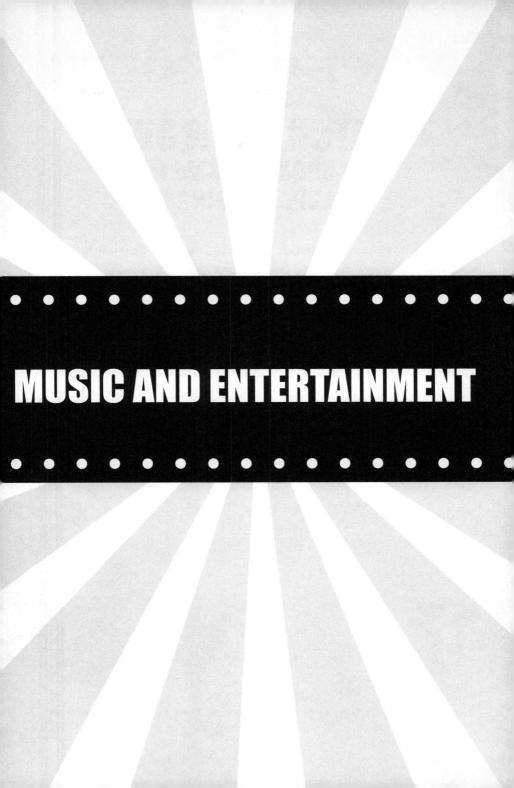

MUSIC AND ENTERTAINMENT

19

WATCH THE MOVIE
AT SPONGEORAMA IN TARPON SPRINGS

Greek immigrants first settled Tarpon Springs as a thriving sponge town, and you'll find that Greek flavor still thriving through the blue and white buildings, small Greek restaurants, and sponges for sale everywhere you look. You'll also find Spongeorama Sponge Factory. This wonderfully odd spot was originally a 1920s sponge-cleaning house. Now, check out the free film that tells the history of sponging in Tarpon Springs through footage from the late '40s and early '70s. (Don't worry, you'll easily find the film in a room adjoining the main shop, thanks to Spongeorama's employees, who really want you to see it.) Once it's over, walk through the small museum with creepy but cool scenes depicting life in a sponging town with mannequins that may be as old as the town itself.

510 Dodecanese Blvd., Tarpon Springs
727-943-2164
spongeorama.com

20

CELEBRATE SUNSET
AT CLEARWATER'S PIER 60

At Clearwater's Pier 60, high-rise hotels and restaurants stretch up and down the beach. Just across the road from the pier are lots of chances to climb aboard boats and head out onto the water in search of dolphins, pirates, or a parasail. And every evening at sunset, the pier transforms itself into a festival. Here, you'll find live music and booths with local artists and crafters. On Friday and Saturday nights, bring a blanket and catch a movie at the beach with the festival's Sunset Cinema, featuring family friendly movies that start at dusk. Buskers also perform most nights, and if you're lucky, you'll find the guy who does a pretty good Captain Jack Sparrow. He'll pose for pictures and has been spotted driving a minivan, admirably staying in character.

10 Pier 60 Dr., Clearwater Beach
sunsetsatpier60.com

CELEBRATE EPIPHANY
IN TARPON SPRINGS

For more than a hundred years, a group of young men have jumped into the cold waters each January in Tarpon Springs, hoping for the sight of a white cross. The tradition is part of Tarpon Springs Epiphany celebrations, presented by St. Nicholas Greek Orthodox Cathedral, which include a blessing of the water, boats, and fishermen. The festivities also include Greek folk dancing, a religious service, and lots of Greek food. Epiphany takes place every year on January 6. You don't have to be part of the community to be part of the celebration, and you don't have to jump in the cold water, either. But while you're there, take time to visit local shops and restaurants and get to know this Greece-meets-Florida town even better.

The church is located at 36 N. Pinellas Ave., Tarpon Springs
727-937-3540
epiphanycity.org

22

DISCOVER THE PERFECT STRAWBERRY SHORTCAKE
IN PLANT CITY

At the annual Florida Strawberry Festival, you'll find live music, games, and lots to see and do. The festival first started in 1930, and it's such an institution that kids in Hillsborough County get a day off each spring to attend. Go for the music, the games, and the festivities, but don't miss the strawberry shortcake. Many restaurants in the area claim to have the best. At the festival, try as many as you can and judge for yourself. While you're there, go check out the adorable animals, the fun rides, the local crafts, and the live entertainment. There's also a strawberry shortcake eating contest, a strawberry stemming contest, a strawberry spaghetti eating contest, and, if you're sick of strawberries, a hot dog eating contest, too.

303 Lemon St., Plant City
813-752-9194
flstrawberryfestival.com

DRESS LIKE A PIRATE
AT GASPARILLA

Kids get Halloween. And if you live in Tampa Bay, in January you get Gasparilla, and you get to dress up like a pirate. You don't have to, of course, but this annual festival celebrates the legendary marauding pirate Jose Gaspar, who is said to have sailed the bay during the 1800s (his actual existence is up for debate). If you've never been, think Mardi Gras with broadswords. There is alcohol. There are floats. There are beads. And yes, it gets a bit wild. For a tamer time, check out the Children's Gasparilla Extravaganza the weekend before. It has all of the fun—including the parade and floats—of the grown-ups' festival, but with a solid PG rating. And, of course, pirate garb is encouraged. If you want to skip the beads and booze, you can still watch the annual invasion of Ye Mystic Krewe of Gasparilla at the Invasion Brunch at the Tampa Convention Center. Tickets cost around sixty dollars for adults and fifty dollars for kids and include great views of this terrific Tampa tradition.

gasparillapiratefest.com

24

SEE THE LIGHTS
IN DOWNTOWN TAMPA

Just before sunset each night, lights begin glowing around the bridges of downtown Tampa. The colors change every thirty seconds through the night with the Agua Luces. You can see the installations by artist Tracey Dear at five of the downtown bridges—CSX Railroad, Platt Street, Brorein Street, Kennedy Street, and the Tampa-Hillsborough Expressway Authority. You can view the lights by car. You can walk from one to the next. You can get on the water by renting an e-Boat, paddle boarding, or booking a bay cruise. You can even can hop on a water taxi for views from below the bridges. Check out Lights on Tampa's site for a full walking tour of this public art you can enjoy downtown after dark.

lightsontampa.org

25

CELEBRATE CIGARS
IN YBOR

Ybor City used to be the home of sprawling cigar factories that were the livelihood of new immigrant communities making Tampa their home. Today, you can still find a good cigar here. Curtains of smoke hang around cigar shops on Ybor City's historic 7th Avenue. Celebrate those cigars with the annual Cigar Heritage Festival in December, where you'll find hand-rolled cigars, live music, food trucks, cigar accessories, and domino tables. The festival hosts a cigar bar crawl in. And you can travel back in time at the Ybor City Museum, which includes a Casita fixed up to show what a cigar worker's home would have looked like during life in the golden days of Cigar City.

yborcitycigarfestival.com

Ybor City Museum, 1818 9th Ave., Tampa
813-247-6323
ybormuseum.org

GO FOR THE MUSIC
AT BUSCH GARDENS

Busch Gardens is known for its wild rides and its wildlife, but you don't have to care about either of those to head to this popular theme park. Instead, go for the music. Busch Gardens has a series of live concerts throughout the year, plus music at the Food and Wine Festival and festivities around the Bier Fest, Howl-O-Scream, and Christmas Town. Check the calendar to see which artists are coming to town for the Real Music, Real Masters series, which has brought music to Tampa since the 1950s. The rides and the animals are still around the park during those events, but there are so many other things to do and see, you could go and totally miss them.

10165 N. McKinley Dr., Tampa
813-884-4386
buschgardens.com/tampa

27

LISTEN TO THE MUSIC

We've got jazz! We've got blues! We've got…Celtic music! Here's a sampling of the music festivals around the bay:

January

Tampa Bay Black Heritage Music Fest, Tampa
tampablackheritage.org

Sunshine Music Festival, St. Petersburg
sunshinemusicfestival.com

February

Music on the Bay, Tampa
musiconthebay.org

Florida State Fair, Tampa
floridastatefair.com

St. Petersburg Jazz Festival, St. Petersburg
stpetejazzfest.com

Clearwater Sea-Blues Festival
myclearwaterevents.com/home

Florida Strawberry Festival, Plant City
flstrawberryfestival.com

Tropical Heatwave, Tampa
tropicalheatwave.org

March

Gasparilla Music Fest, Tampa, gasparillamusic.com

April

Tampa Bay Blues Festival, St. Petersburg
tampabaybluesfest.com

Safety Harbor Songfest, Safety Harbor
safetyharborsongfest.com

Tampa Bay Caribbean Carnival, Tampa
tampabaycaribbeancarnival.com

June

Rays Summer Concert Series, St. Petersburg
mlb.com/rays

Opa! Palooza Greek Festival, Tarpon Springs
spongedocks.net

October

Clearwater Jazz Holiday, Clearwater
clearwaterjazz.com

Harbor Sounds, Safety Harbor
safetyharborchamber.com

John's Pass Seafood and Music Festival, Madeira Beach
johnspassseafoodfest.com

November

Suncoast Jazz Classic, Clearwater
suncoastjazzfestival.com

Dunedin Wines the Blues, Dunedin
dunedingov.com

Dunedin Celtic Music & Craft Beer Festival, Dunedin
dunedincelticmusicfestival.com

Ribfest, St. Petersburg
ribfest.org

Conga Caliente, Tampa
congacaliente.com

December

Bradenton Blues Festival, Bradenton

LISTEN TO THE SUNSET BELL

AT PASS-A-GRILLE BEACH

Florida has something like 660 miles of beach, and many beaches claim to be the best. You should judge that for yourself. Some, like Fort De Soto, feel remote and a bit wild. Some, like Clearwater's Pier 60, are polished, paved, and could be the setting for a spring break movie, bikini-clad rollerbladers and all. But Pass-A-Grille Beach, in the town of St. Pete Beach, is the perfect mix of civilization and sand. Near sunset, find a spot to watch the sun sink into the water. At the Hurricane Seafood Restaurant, head to the rooftop for postcard views. Or go across the street to the beachfront Paradise Grille. If you get there early enough, take up one of the worn Adirondacks. When the sun finally sinks into the sea, a Grille employee chooses one person to give the "Sunset Bell" a good clang. Actually, it's fifteen good clangs. According to Gulf Beaches Historical Museum, the bell—which has been at that spot since the late 1990s—gets five rings to remind the sea gulls to fly home to nearby Shell Island, five rings to honor the ringer, and five rings to honor the tradition.

The Hurricane Seafood Restaurant, 809 Gulf Way, St. Pete Beach
727-360-9558, thehurricane.com

Paradise Grille, 900 Gulf Way, St. Pete Beach
727-367-1495, facebook.com/paradisegrillePAG

TIP

Pass-A-Grille, on the National Register of Historic Places, has more to see than just the beach, including the very short but store-filled Eighth Avenue. Off Gulf Boulevard, you'll also find Corey Avenue, a longer street lined with shops and restaurants.

29

WATCH LEGOS SKI
IN WINTER HAVEN

Many people over a certain age remember Cypress Gardens, with its vast stretches of manicured green lawns, the daring ski show, and the belles in hoop skirts who wandered the grounds after the shows ended. That space is now Legoland Florida, but the past is still very present here. A corner of the grounds celebrates Cypress Gardens' past and includes an old Cypress tree with limbs dripping to the ground in all directions (plus a large, hoop-skirted Lego belle). If you want to get a sense of what the ski shows were like, that's not too hard either. They still happen every day in what's now called "Pirate's Cove." There, you'll find a daring ski show featuring, yes, people dressed up as Legos.

One Legoland Way, Winter Haven
877-350-5346
legoland.com/florida

30

SEE ORLANDO FROM ABOVE

People come to Orlando from all over the world for the Disney parks, the Universal parks, and SeaWorld. But this vacation destination also has something in common with cities including Chicago, London, and Las Vegas—a giant Ferris wheel. ICON Orlando is an observation wheel that glides into the air offering views of swamps, theme parks, homes, and businesses across Central Florida. There's a bar at the base where you can get drinks for the ride, which takes a little more than twenty minutes. And inside, digital guides help you figure out what you're seeing from up so high. If you time it right, you can catch the sunset or the Disney Parks fireworks shows and get a one-of-a-kind view of a one-of-a-kind place.

8445 International Dr., Orlando
iconorlando.com

FIND THE MERMAIDS
AT WEEKI WACHEE SPRINGS

Once you've taken a swim in the clear blue cold springs at Weeki Wachee Springs State Park, you'll appreciate the hard-working mermaids here. They've been performing since 1947, and they twist and turn, slipping their hookah-like oxygen tubes around them as they perform. It is not Broadway underwater, but the play of light, the floating hair, and the shimmering tails make for a great show. They perform *The Little Mermaid*, of course, and a show that includes a set of tricks such as eating and drinking underwater. The shows are also a great chance to wildlife watch, with turtles and fish making regular guest appearances. After you've seen the mermaids, rent a tube and float the lazy river at Buccaneer Bay. You can also enjoy water slides and a river boat cruise that's included with admission.

6131 Commercial Way, Spring Hill
352-592-5656
weekiwachee.com

32

VISIT A GIANT BIRTHDAY CAKE ON THE BEACH

AT THE DON CESAR

The Loews Don CeSar sits on the St. Pete Beach skyline like a giant, pink-frosted birthday cake. This luxurious hotel was built in 1928, but you don't have to stay there to enjoy the "Pink Palace." Like the Vinoy in St. Petersburg, the Don hosted an Army hospital during World War II. It was restored and reopened as a hotel in the 1970s. Now you can stop by this jewel on the National Register of Historic Places for resort-style shopping at the basement level, or try one of several restaurants. If you sit outside at the Sea Porch Cafe, you'll get views of blue water ahead of you and pink hotel behind you.

3400 Gulf Blvd., St. Pete Beach
727-360-1881
doncesar.com

SPORTS AND RECREATION

CLIMB THROUGH THE OLD OAKS
AT MEDARD PARK IN PLANT CITY

Edward Medard Conservation Park used to be a phosphate mine. Now, you'll find fishing, camping, horseback riding, and, if you know where to look, a forest of above-ground tree roots. It costs two dollars cash to get into this sprawling county park. Take your second left onto Sacred Hills Drive. Then, look to your right. There, hidden in a cloud of green leaves, are mini root mountains towering up from the ground like something from a movie. Our seasonal rains and silty soil caused the erosion that exposed the oak tree roots, which stretch out as far as you can see in both directions. It can get slippery if there's been a lot of rain, so wear good shoes. But thanks to the elements, you can climb the hills and explore this root jungle.

6140 Turkey Creek Rd., Plant City
813-757-3802
hillsboroughcounty.org/en/locations

MAXIMUM CAPACITIES
5 PERSONS OR 715 LBS

34

CANOE THE ALAFIA

Tampa Bay has a lot of places to kayak and canoe, and if you live here, you probably have a favorite. If it's not already, the Alafia River should be one of them. You can rent a canoe for twenty-five dollars for the day from the family-owned Alafia River Canoe Rentals, which has sent people onto the water for more than forty years. Day-long trips are best in the spring, when the water is low, and you can head out from the dock and explore for the day. You can also let the current take you to a boat ramp downstream, where they'll pick you up. But make sure to call first. The water, like the weather, is unpredictable.

4419 River Dr., Valrico
813-689-8645

MEET RESCUED BIRDS AND WILD ONES
AT SEASIDE SEABIRD SANCTUARY

The birds are everywhere—in the trees, around the entrance, perched atop the A-framed cages. Pull into the parking lot or shuffle up from the beach and you'll find between thirty and forty species at the small but busy Seaside Seabird Sanctuary in Indian Shores. Remember, as you watch the pelicans, herons, eagles, and hawks, that this is a home for birds, not people. Your nose will confirm that. The rescued birds are in huts or behind fences, but you'll see wild birds, too, including huge, fierce-looking vultures perched in a spindly tree that come here, according to staff, because there's safety in numbers, and this place has numbers. The free admission includes daily pelican hand-feeding demonstrations and twice-weekly screech owl presentations.

18328 Gulf Blvd., Indian Shores
727-391-6211
seabirdsanctuary.com

TAKE A WALK
ALONG BAYSHORE BOULEVARD

Hugging the city and the bay, Bayshore Boulevard offers long views of both along 4.5 miles of sidewalks in Tampa. Walking here you'll see grand, historic homes, Tampa's jagged skyline, and the sparkling waters of Tampa Bay. You can also jog, bike, skate, and scoot along what the City of Tampa says is the world's longest continuous sidewalk. Bayshore Boulevard included a trolley when it was first established in the 1890s, according to the Cultural Landscape Foundation, and it's been part of Tampa's Greenway trail since 1989. Try Bayshore Linear Park Trail for a spot to leave your car and hit the road. If you travel the entire boulevard, you'll pass several parks. Look for the bronze trail markers in the sidewalk that mark the distance.

312 Bayshore Blvd., Tampa
tampagov.net/parks-and-recreation

37

SWIM WITH THE SHARKS
AT THE FLORIDA AQUARIUM

You could stand in front of the 500,000-gallon tank on the second floor of the Florida Aquarium for hours, watching the sand tiger shark or the giant sea turtle or the twisting eel. Or you could just dive in. Certified scuba divers age fifteen and over can swim in the Coral Reef Exhibit with a dive master for $175, which includes admission and a photo. You can also swim with the sand tiger sharks (no scuba certification needed) for $110. The guides offer assurances that the sharks are well fed and have no interest in the divers, but if you'd rather watch from outside the water, just seeing them glide close by is still fun. And if you really don't want to be near the sharks, head outside to the Splash Pad, a watery playground perfect for your minnows.

701 Channelside Dr., Tampa
813-273-4000
flaquarium.org

TIP

Since you're already so close, head over to Channelside Bay Plaza, where you'll find restaurants, shops, and lots of spots for people watching (particularly cruise-goer people watching).

38

TAKE IN THE VIEW
ON THE SUNSHINE SKYWAY

Florida doesn't have many mountains or hills, but you can certainly get closer to the clouds on a trip over the Bob Graham Sunshine Skyway Bridge. Crossing from one side to the next (after paying the toll) is a fast trip, marked by the passing stripes of yellow cables that stretch down each side and stand out from a distance. You can't stop for photos, of course, and traffic moves fast, so you probably won't even get to slow down. But heading both on and off the bridge, you can get great views of Tampa Bay from great heights. While you're heading there, remember to bring your rod and your fishing gear and visit parts of the old Skyway Bridge that are now the Skyway Fishing Pier State Park. It's open year round.

39

SEE TAMPA BAY'S SKYLINES
AT APOLLO BEACH

This Hillsborough County park has two acres of sand, water, and city views. From the preserve, you can see the skylines of both Tampa and St. Petersburg. Bonus—you can bring your dog. Warning—lots of people do just that. Thanks to how close it is to the Big Bend Power Station, there's a good chance you'll also spot some manatees headed to or from their manmade winter spa. (If you want to see even more wildlife, head over to nearby E. G. Simmons Regional Park in Ruskin for birdwatching.) Apollo Beach Nature Preserve, which has free but limited parking, also has a covered picnic area and restrooms. It's open from sunrise to sunset.

6760 Surfside Blvd., Apollo Beach
813-672-7876
hillsboroughcounty.org/en/locations

HUNT FOR SHARK TEETH
IN VENICE

Don't be nervous. The teeth you'll be hunting in Venice aren't with the sharks anymore, but with a little patience you can still dig them up at the beaches here. South of Sarasota, Venice is about an hour or so drive from Tampa. In April, the city hosts the Shark's Tooth Festival, where these prehistoric fossils are available for sale. The festival also has food, artists, and live music. But you don't have to wait until April to get your own shark's teeth. At most beaches, just rent a basket that helps you sift through the sand and shells. It's not easy, maybe a bit like panning for gold, but it's so worth it when you come upon a pointy prehistoric treasure.

sharkstoothfest.com

41

LISTEN TO THE MOB
AT A ROWDIES GAME

You'll probably go to Al Lang Stadium in St. Petersburg to watch Tampa Bay's professional soccer team, the Rowdies. While you're there, Ralph's Mob, the team's official supporters, offer a pretty great side show. They sing, they drum, they chant. And you can join in, or just sit back and enjoy their team spirit. Like devoted soccer fans around the world, this group brings wild excitement to the stadium before, during, and after the game. They also hold several charity drives a year for the community. Soccer isn't yet as popular in the United States as it is in the rest of the world. But you'd never know it when watching Ralph's Mob. Check their website for a list of chants and songs and "sing a song for Tampa Bay."

230 1st St. South, St. Petersburg
727-222-2000
rowdiessoccer.com

SEE A PREHISTORIC CANOE

AT WEEDON ISLAND PRESERVE

Explore more than 3,000 acres of nature at this preserve that was once home to indigenous people. Even better, see the 1,100-year-old canoe in the Welcome Center. Nearly forty feet long, it was discovered several years ago at the preserve. While here, view exhibits that will help you get to know more about the prehistoric people who lived here for hundreds of years. Then, trade in your driver's license for a backpack with binoculars, a magnifying glass, and an Audubon bird guide. You can hike, paddle, fish, or take to the stroller-friendly boardwalks through dense tangles of mangroves. Peek inside for birds, fish, and crabs, and imagine what life was like for the people who once paddled that canoe.

1800 Weedon Dr. Northeast, St. Petersburg
727-453-6500
weedonislandpreserve.org

43

EXPLORE THE RUINS
AT EGMONT KEY

Catch the Tampa Bay Ferry at Hubbard's Marina in Fort De Soto Park to reach this secluded island that has played a key role in history, including during the Civil War and the Spanish-American War. On the island you'll find the remains of Fort Dade, the perfect place to enjoy a beach-front adventure. You can climb the steps and explore the ruins of the old fort. Egmont Key also features a lighthouse that's more than 150 years old and six miles of paths that allow you to get from one end to the other. But come prepared—Egmont Key does not have a store, restrooms, or running water.

352-563-2088
floridastateparks.org/park/Egmont-Key

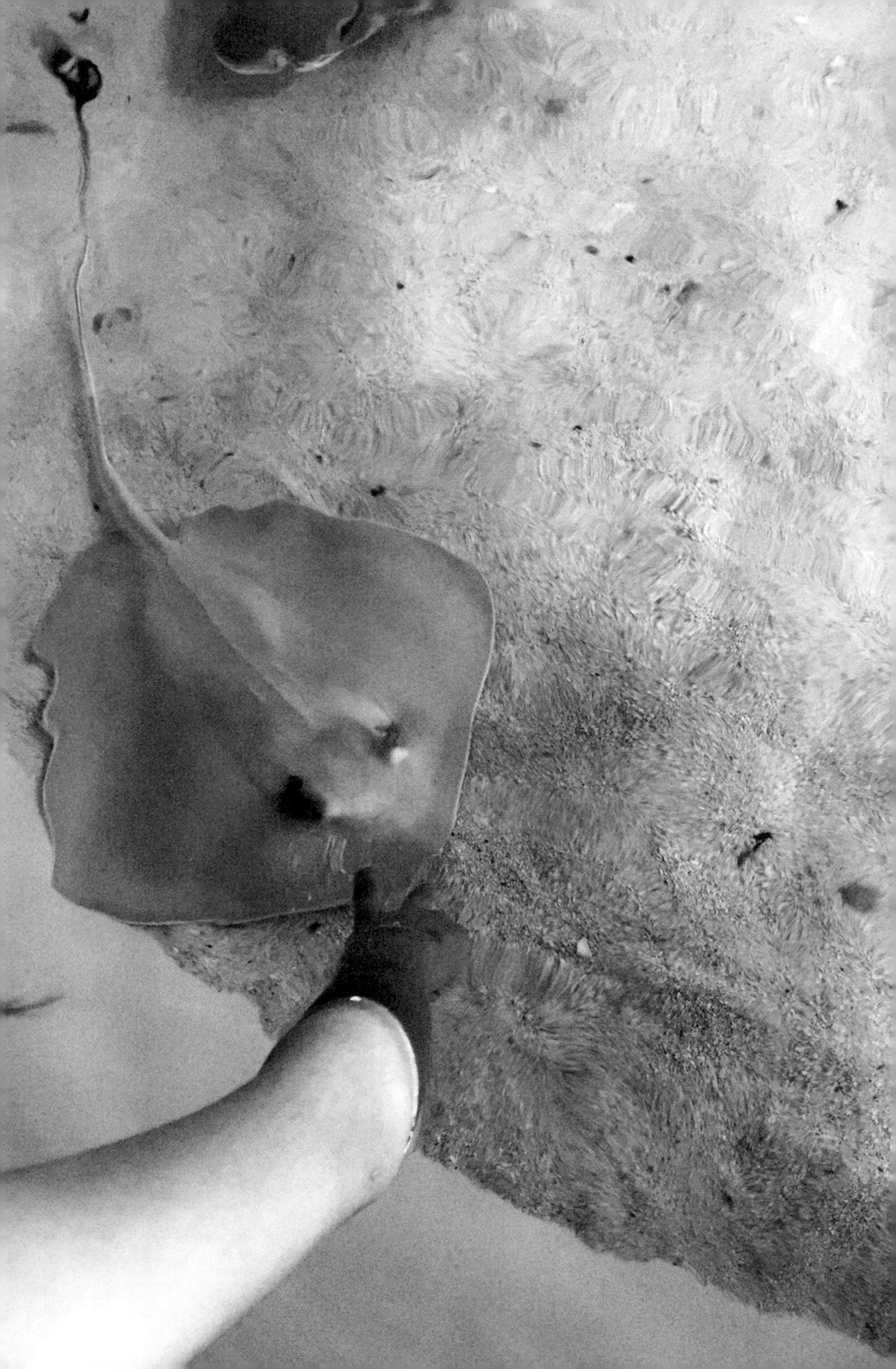

SEE THE MANATEES (AND THE RAYS) AT BIG BEND

When the temperatures drop enough to make the locals start to shiver (around 68 degrees, seriously), head for the tall smokestacks that stretch into the skyline at Apollo Beach. Where Big Bend Power Station releases warm, clean saltwater into the bay, manatees gather to get cozy at this federally designated manatee sanctuary. It's like a spa for sea cows. The Manatee Viewing Center is totally free, and unlike other places where you can see manatees, here, they come and go as they please. That means you have to wait until the temps are cold—by Floridian standards, at least—to see them up close. After watching the manatees, take a stroll on the tidal walk. Through a canopy of mangroves, you can spot local fish, birds, plants, and crustaceans. In the winter, you'll also get to pet the stingrays that are on break from their baseball home at Tampa Bay Rays' Tropicana Field.

6990 Dickman Rd., Apollo Beach
813-228-4289
tampaelectric.com/company/mvc

45

MEET SOME UNLIKELY ROOMMATES
AT BIG CAT RESCUE

Hiding between a mall and a gas station, the long, private road that leads to Big Cat Rescue feels remote, like you're heading into the wild the farther you go. And in a lot of ways, you are. Inside the home of this nonprofit, you'll find more than a hundred big cats that have been rescued from some pretty horrific situations. Make sure to look for the oddly paired Cameron and Zabu. Cameron, a male African lion, and Zabu, a female Bengal tiger, share their space because they've been together since they were babies. During the week, most tours are for people age ten and up, but all kids (and their parents) can enjoy special tours on the weekends, so check the schedule first. And depending on the weather (and the season), you might need closed-toed shoes or even good boots. The road gets pretty muddy, but the cats don't seem to mind.

12802 Easy St., Tampa
813-920-4130
bigcatrescue.org

TAKE IN THE VIEW
AT FORT DE SOTO

Unlike a lot of the beaches in Tampa Bay, at Fort De Soto Park, the skyline's just sky. You won't see any high-rises. You won't see any condos. You'll just see blue water and blue horizon. The area, which was first the home of Tocobaga Indians, played a role in defense during both the Civil War and the Spanish-American War. The actual fort was finished in 1900, and you can see what remains today for yourself. Visit the beach here, for sure, which feels quiet and remote. And before you head back to the concrete and traffic, climb the steep stone steps up to the top of the fort and enjoy the uninterrupted views of Tampa Bay.

3500 Pinellas Bay Way South, Tierra Verde
727-582-2267
pinellascounty.org/park

WALK ON WATER
AT LETTUCE LAKE PARK

At this Hillsborough County Park, a wooden walkway takes you out into the swamp. You'll walk along a boardwalk that twists through vegetation that's home to wild birds, alligators, and more. Head to the towering lookout leading up a few stories for views of the Hillsborough River that only the birds get. And look for signs along the way that tell you about all the wildlife you're seeing. If you want even more detail, join one of the park's regular native plant and bird walks. Entry into this 240-acre park costs two dollars per car. There's lots of free parking, several restrooms, picnic shelters, and a playground.

6920 E. Fletcher Ave., Tampa
813-987-6204
hillsboroughcounty.org/locations

48

SEE WINTER THE DOLPHIN

Next to Shamu and Willy, not many sea creatures get their own movies (or sequels). But this dolphin that was rescued by a fisherman and given a prosthetic tail really is a star. Winter, and her trainers, will show you how she's doing each day, and seeing her for yourself is way better than any movie. The Clearwater Marine Aquarium is an animal hospital and home to other sea life on the mend, including stingrays, sharks, sea turtles, pelicans, and otters. While there, go see Winter's real-life co-star, Hope, another rescued dolphin. The aquarium puts on a number of demonstrations each day. If you need a Winter fix and can't make it to the aquarium, go to the live web cams to check in with her, Hope, and several other aquarium residents.

249 Windward Passage, Clearwater
727-441-1790
seewinter.com

SEE SOME BIG LIZARDS
AT DINOSAUR WORLD

Dinosaur World in Plant City can feel a bit, well, post-prehistoric as you make your way through the gift shop and dino-themed playground. Keep going. Once you hit the cover of trees, things get very cool, very fast. Out from the deep Florida green, dinosaurs lurk fierce and tall. Follow the path to a giant sandbox, where parents can take a break while kids dig for bones. Keep going and you'll discover a skeleton garden and a long wooden boardwalk teeming with carnivores. The canopy makes this a great place to visit pretty much any time. And bring along a picnic—you'll find several shady spots that may include some brave, and well-fed, squirrels, which can be much scarier than the dinos.

5145 Harvey Tew Rd., Plant City
813-717-9865
dinosaurworld.com

LEAVE THE CITY BEHIND
AT SUNKEN GARDENS

This hushed and lush spot sits on busy 4th Street North in St. Pete, but from inside the Sunken Gardens, you'd never guess it. You'll find several acres of tropical greenery here that began in 1903 when a plumber drained a lake on his property and started planting. It opened as Turner's Sunken Gardens in 1935, and in 1999, the City of St. Pete bought the local historic landmark. Head there today (look for the bright, retro sign on the street) and take off down paved paths packed with fragrant green growth. Down those paths, you'll find koi ponds, pink flamingos, and many places to sit and pretend you are in the rain forest and not, really, in the middle of a city.

1825 4th St. North, St. Petersburg
727-551-3102,

51

PLAY WITH THE RAYS
AT TROPICANA FIELD

If you've never been to Tropicana Field before, do not turn around and leave once you get inside. You're in the right place. It is not a circus. Along with watching the Tampa Bay Rays play ball, you'll find a lot of fun things to do inside this indoor stadium. The Rays have family fun days every Sunday when they're in town for home games. If your little ones can't sit still until the seventh inning stretch, head to Left Field Street to buy baseball cards and jerseys with your name on them. Center Field Street offers restaurants where you can eat while watching the game. And at Right Field Street, kiddos can take a swing in the batting cage and color pictures of mascot Raymond (he's a "seadog"). At Sunday games, kids under fourteen can also run the bases. You can't do that at the circus.

1 Tropicana Field, St. Petersburg
727-825-3137
mlb.com/rays

52

PLAY SHUFFLEBOARD

Shuffleboard is kind of a Florida cliché—think retirees in Hawaiian shirts and visors. It's also really fun. The St. Pete Shuffleboard Club has players of all ages who embrace the sport's history in their own ways. The club, which turns ninety-five in 2019, hosts St. Pete Shuffle every Friday night from 7 to 11 p.m. with live music and food trucks. There's also an annual tweed bicycle ride, which looks as cool as it sounds. If you haven't tried shuffleboard yet, the club offers boot camps. Once you're comfortable, you can form or join a league for league nights. Shuffleboard may be a Florida cliché, but the way they play it here, it feels like a refreshing approach to a classic.

559 Mirror Lake Dr. North, St. Petersburg
727-882-2083
stpeteshuffle.com

STROLL THE RIVERWALK

The trolley and the streetcar are fun options for getting around downtown Tampa, if they're running. But one of your best bets for exploring is your own two feet. The Tampa Riverwalk stretches for two miles along the Hillsborough River and includes frequent signs to make sure you know where you are. It will take you from the Florida Aquarium to the Tampa Bay History Center (visit the Columbia Restaurant while you're there), then to the dancing fountains at Curtis Hixon Waterfront Park. Stop by the Tampa Art Museum, stroll past the Straz, where you can stop and enjoy art installations, and keep going all the way to Water Works Park, where your small travelers can cool off at the splash park. Along the way, you'll find restaurants, history, and a different perspective of downtown Tampa.

thetampariverwalk.com

54

CLIMB THE PORTAVANT TEMPLE MOUND

Hidden among green growth at Emerson Point Preserve sits Tampa Bay's largest Amerindian temple mound. The spot, which dates back more than a thousand years, was the site of religious ceremonies. It was built up, bit by bit, over time with pieces of shells, pottery, and discarded bones. Today, discovering it is an easy walk. Follow the signs and climb up a ramp to the top. The mound is covered in vegetation now, but signs along the way will help you get to know more about the Amerindians, what their lives were like, and why they built the mounds in the first place. While you're there, discover great views at Emerson Point Preserve. This park is full of great trails for walking, hiking, and riding, plus plenty of picnic spots. On one of those trails, a boardwalk takes you over water, past mangroves, and into great views. From a lookout tower, you can see where the Manatee River meets Tampa Bay, as well as the bright yellow arms of the Sunshine Skyway Bridge in the distance.

5801 17th St. West, Palmetto
mymanatee.org/departments/parks___natural_resources

GET A DIFFERENT VIEW OF TAMPA
FROM THE WATER

You may not be lucky enough to own your own boat, so go ahead and rent something that will get you on the water. Near the Tampa Convention Center, you can rent an eBoat, like a golf cart on the water. You only need a driver's license and up to nine friends to drive one of the covered boats through downtown Tampa. If that's not your speed, or size, hop into a mini powerboat. And if you'd like to take things much more slowly, and burn a lot more calories, try Tampa Bay Water Bike Co.'s water bikes, which are really like bikes but on water. However you do it, get on the water for a different way to explore Tampa.

Tampa Convention Center
333 S. Franklin St., Tampa

eBoats Tampa
813-767-2245
eboatstampa.com

Riverwalk Boating Company
813-641-4612
riverwalkboating.com

Tampa Bay Water Bike Co.
813-465-8025
tampawaterbikes.com

250
250

BOAT TO BEER CAN ISLAND

It's officially called Pine Key, but if you live in Tampa Bay, it's Beer Can Island. Boat up to this spot near Apollo Beach for shelling, fishing, swimming, and secluded fun. Walk around the entire island and look for tangles of washed up, bleached out trees that are great for climbing. If that's all a bit too remote for you, a manmade island exists right nearby—Tiki Bay Island. The owners of the 2,400-square-foot floating bar also own Beer Can Island. You can stop by Tiki Bay for food and drinks and to rent kayaks and paddle boards. You can visit Beer Can Island for free, but if you want to use the restrooms or camp overnight, get passes from Tiki Bay. The only way to get to the island is by boat, so you'll have to rent one or get to know people who own one.

tikibayisland.com

WATCH CARS RACE
THROUGH DOWNTOWN ST. PETE

Every spring, Indy cars take over downtown St. Pete for a few days when the streets turn into race tracks at the Firestone Grand Prix of St. Petersburg. You can watch the fast-moving action from the water if you have a yacht or a whole lot of money. You can get tickets to the race. Or you can take to buildings and parking garages along the route, if you can get to them, for a peek at the action. The race isn't just about the cars—there's also a festival, food, a movie, and a 5K. The Indy cars go by fast, but the weekend offers lots of chances to shift gears and enjoy the race, the festivities, and the city that shifts to make room for them.

gpstpete.com

GO MOUNTAIN BIKING
AT ALAFIA RIVER STATE PARK

Alafia River State Park will make you forget flat Florida, at least for a little while. The park, built on an old phosphate mine, has twenty miles of bike trails that mountain bikers love, but it also has some easier trails for those who aren't quite so skilled. Each November, the park is the site of the Alafia Fat Tire Festival, named among the best fests by *Outside* magazine several years ago. You can also join SWAMP Mountain Bike Club for weekly rides that will help you get to know the terrain, and the people on it, even better. If you want to keep your feet a bit closer to the ground, the park has twenty miles of hiking trails that are shared by people enjoying the park on horseback. You can also camp, kayak, and canoe here.

14326 S. County Rd. 39, Lithia
813-672-5320
floridastateparks.org/park/Alafia-River

swampclub.org

GO SHELLING
AT SHELL KEY

This barrier island is a wildlife preserve and a spot for "nesting and resting," according to the Great Florida Birding and Wildlife Trail website. But you'll probably want to visit for the shelling. Shell Key is a remote spot, meaning there aren't bathrooms, running water, or any places to buy the things you may have forgotten, so pack well. Want to visit? The Shell Key Shuttle will get you there. The shuttle leaves from St. Pete Beach for Shell Key three times a day. Admission includes the boat ride, an umbrella, a mask, and a snorkel. The shells are free—you just have to find them. If a day isn't enough time, plan ahead and bring your camping gear. You need a camping permit to stay at Shell Key, and they're available from Pinellas County.

801 Pass-A-Grille Way, St. Pete Beach
727-360-1348
shellkey.org

shellkeyshuttle.com

SEE (INSERT YOUR TEAM HERE)
AT SPRING TRAINING

Tampa Bay fills up with all kinds of people when the temps cool down elsewhere. Among them—Major League Baseball players. Teams in the Grapefruit League around this region include the New York Yankees in Tampa, the Pittsburgh Pirates in Bradenton, the Baltimore Orioles in Sarasota, the Detroit Tigers in Lakeland, the Philadelphia Phillies in Clearwater, and the Toronto Blue Jays in Dunedin. If your team isn't training in Tampa Bay, check the schedule to see if they'll be in town playing one of the teams close by. The big leagues have called Florida their spring home for more than 125 years, and while the fields and stadiums are much smaller, that just means the games and the players are that much closer.

floridagrapefruitleague.com

61

FISH (OR JUST WATCH THE FISH)
AT THE ROD AND REEL PIER ON ANNA MARIA

This pier, restaurant, and bar sits at the north end of beautiful Anna Maria Island, under a hand-painted sign, over a long wooden walkway out onto the water. At this island institution, which is more than seventy years old, there's a bar downstairs, a restaurant upstairs, and fantastic water views all around. There are also lots of people ready to fish. Bring your fishing pole, buy a bucket of live shrimp, and watch fish, including black and white sheepshead, take the bait. Look for dolphins as you wait for the fish to bite, or just people watch. But keep an eye on the pelicans, cranes, and other shore birds. They do not come for the fantastic views.

875 N. Shore Dr., Anna Maria
941-778-1885
rodreelpier.com

BEACH BUMS
OCEAN KAYAK

62

HOP THE FERRY

TO CALADESI ISLAND

Even though it's visible from several spots in Tampa Bay, the only way to get to Caladesi Island is by boat. That trip takes you through spindly tangles of red mangroves and drops you at the state park, where you can grab something to eat, any beach gear you may have forgotten, and some very necessary bug spray. A short walk away (look out for resident eastern diamondback rattlesnakes), you're at a quiet stretch of undisturbed beach. There's also camping, fishing, picnicking, three miles of hiking trails, three miles of kayaking, and a playground. The ferry to Caladesi Island leaves from Honeymoon Island State Park several times a day.

#1 Causeway Blvd., Dunedin
727-734-5263
caladesiferry.org
floridastateparks.org/park/Caladesi-Island

SEE THE BARANOFF OAK TREE
IN SAFETY HARBOR

This live oak at 2nd and Main in Safety Harbor is between three hundred and five hundred years old, according to the city, and it was named after the doctor who owned the famous Safety Harbor Resort and Spa. It's thought to be the oldest oak in Pinellas County. Admire its giant trunk and great winding branches that could be trees all by themselves. While you're in town, head over to the Safety Harbor Library to see the Elf Tree, a two-hundred-year-old live oak that was grown on top of an Indian shell mound and looks like it's about to climb out of the earth. There's also Pipkin Oak, which sits in Art Park and was named for another influential resident of the town. The oaks' names honor the history of the town, but just looking at them, you'll appreciate how short a time that really was compared with the lives of these majestic trees.

101 2nd Ave. North, Safety Harbor
727-724-1558
cityofsafetyharbor.com/389/Parks

SEE REAL LIGHTNING
AT A LIGHTNING GAME

You won't just see Tampa's hockey-playing Lightning at Tampa's downtown Amalie Arena. When you go for an NHL game, you'll also see the real stuff. Two Tesla coils hang from the ceiling and get fired up before the game and every time the Lightning score. Along with the chants, cheering, clapping, and booming music, fans can see and hear real fingers of lightning zapping and crackling. If you're taking the whole family, look for family pack tickets, which include food and drinks. Want to send those bright bolts out yourself? Contact group sales, and you can play Zeus during the second intermission. And don't worry. Florida is the lightning capital of North America. But inside this stadium, you'll only be struck with awe.

401 Channelside Dr., Tampa
813-301-6500
lightning.nhl.com

CLIMB ABOARD THE PIRATE SHIP
AT RAYMOND JAMES STADIUM

Tampa has a few famous pirate ships. You've likely seen the legendary *Jose Gasparilla*, which "invades" the bay each year for Gasparilla, with a rowdy and swashbuckling crew that demands the key to the city. But there's another one. In the North End Zone at Raymond James Stadium, a 103-foot pirate ship sits landlocked year round. During games, the ship at Buccaneer Cove fires cannons when the Tampa Bay Buccaneers score a field goal or a touchdown. You can't watch the game from the bow, but you can tour it when the Bucs aren't playing. During the week, join a seventy-five-minute walking tour and see the locker room, the field, and, aye, that big pirate ship that's moored in a football field's end zone.

4201 N. Dale Mabry, Tampa
813-350-6500
raymondjamesstadium.com/stadium-tours

CLIMB INTO THE TREES
AT THE MARIE SELBY BOTANICAL GARDENS

In Sarasota, the Ann Goldstein Children's Rainforest Garden uses a very old tree for very good fun. The children's area at the seventy-five-year-old Marie Selby Botanical Gardens winds up into a fig tree first planted in the 1920s. You can run around the tree, climb up into lookout towers in the branches, and head back down again. A waterfall and a canyon beckon. At the Amazon village, you can drum and build or just swing back for a little while and appreciate the natural beauty in the hammock seats nearby. Just by the Rainforest Garden, a huge Banyan tree offers massive snaky, windy roots that are perfect for climbing up, on, over, and around.

900 S. Palm Ave., Sarasota
941-366-5731
selby.org

SWIM WITH THE MANATEES
AT CRYSTAL RIVER

Tampa Bay boasts several places to see manatees, but at Crystal River, you can be with the manatees. In the water! This beautiful spot is about an hour and a half drive north of Tampa. Several operators will take you to the right spot for manatee co-swimming, including the postcard-esque Three Sisters Springs. They'll provide a wet suit, which you'll need because the water is a crisp seventy-two degrees Fahrenheit year round. In the hotter months (half the year), that will feel refreshing, but you won't see a lot of manatees. When it's cooler outside, by Florida standards, the manatees head to the springs to stay warm. But you don't have to swim with the manatees to enjoy the springs. You can rent kayaks or stroll the four-and-a-half-mile boardwalk. Whether you're in the water, on the water, or watching the water, the views are spectacular.

123 N.W. US 19, Crystal River
352-586-1170
threesistersspringsvisitor.org

TIP

If you don't see many, or any, manatees, visit them at Ellie Schiller Homosassa Springs Wildlife State Park, which has an underwater observatory.

4150 S. Suncoast Blvd., Homosassa
352-628-5543
floridastateparks.org/park/Homosassa-Springs

SEE ALL THE HOLIDAY LIGHTS

You have so many options here. Join one of many holiday lights cruises (often with singalong and hot cocoa) at Tampa's Riverwalk. Head to Busch Gardens for its annual Christmas Town, which sparkles with thousands of lights and several holiday-themed shows. There's a Chick-Fil-A on Waters Avenue in Tampa that's put on a headline-worthy show for nearly twenty years. In St. Pete, walk through the elaborate Oakdale display. It's more than forty years old and has half a million lights. In Orlando, head to the Gaylord Palms for the grand hotel's holiday offerings, including a light show and sledding. And you can walk down Christmas Tree Trail at Disney Springs in Orlando and see the Disney movie-themed trees. If one of those doesn't sprinkle some cheer into your holidays, perhaps only the Grinch can help you.

River of Lights Holiday Cruises
333 S. Franklin, Tampa
813- 390-3711
piratewatertaxi.com

Busch Gardens
10165 N. McKinley Dr., Tampa
813-884-4386
buschgardens.com

Chick-Fil-A
6299 W. Waters Ave., Tampa
813-880-0808
thechickenwire.chick-fil-a.com/Inside-Chick-fil-A/Slide-show-Tampa-Winter-Wonderland

Oakdale Christmas Display
2719 Oakdale St. South, St. Petersburg
christmasdisplay.org

Gaylord Palms
6000 W. Osceola Parkway, Kissimmee
407-586-0000
marriott.com/hotels/travel/mcogp-gaylord-palms-resort-and-convention-center

Disney Springs
1486 Buena Vista Dr., Orlando
disneysprings.org

69

DIP INTO LITHIA SPRINGS

Tucked in at the end of a rural road, Lithia Springs Conservation Park has the cold, cold water Florida springs are famous for. Unlike a lot of other natural springs, though, this one's not too far from home. The 160-acre site has campsites, picnic spots, and a large, fenced-off swimming hole. It's located in Lithia, which is about forty-minutes from downtown Tampa and an hour from downtown St. Pete. It costs two dollars per car, and two dollars per person to swim. If you're planning a visit during the summer, plan to arrive early. The springs fill up fast on hot summer days thanks to that cold, cold water, and once it's at capacity, you'll have to enjoy the sight of the springs, not the feel of it.

3932 Lithia Springs Rd., Lithia
813-774-5572
hillsboroughcounty.org/locations

STROLL GULFPORT

This small town on Boca Ciega Bay is full of quirky charm. Before you park and start your stroll, drive up and down the roads of Gulfport and discover the brightly painted bungalows lining the streets. Next, head to Beach Boulevard, find a spot, and start walking. Numerous shops filled with treasures from local artists line the boulevard, as well as small restaurants where you can sit outside under the shade and sip something cool. If you're hungry, try one of the many waterfront staples on Shore Boulevard. If you want a little more action, come for the Art Walk on the first Friday and third Saturday of each month, or wait for the end of the summer and GeckoFest. While you're in town, peek into Gulfport's Casino Ballroom. It's now used mostly for private events, but the 1930s historic landmark is also the site of weekly dance classes, if you're up for a little bit more than a stroll.

gulfportflorida.us

CULTURE AND HISTORY

71

FIND AN OLD LOVE STORY
AT OAKLAWN CEMETERY

This downtown Tampa cemetery, which first opened in 1850, was a place for "white and slave, rich and poor," according to the City of Tampa. Today, it's full of tall trees draped in Spanish moss and aging headstones that tell many interesting stories about the city. There are government figures, businessmen, slaves, and pirates. And there's a love story. Look for the headstone of William and Nancy Ashley, a prominent white resident and the African American servant who was thought to be his partner. Their gravestone reads "Here lies Wm. Ashley and Nancy Ashley, Master, and Servant. Faithful to each other in that relation in life, in death they are not seperated *(sic)*. Stranger consider and be wiser. In the grave, all human distinction, of race or caste, mingle together in one common dust." The city of Tampa offers a self-guided walking tour, which you can find online.

606 E. Harrison St., Tampa
tampagov.net/parks-and-recreation/cemeteries/oaklawn-walking-tour

72

GET SPOOKED
ON AN YBOR CITY GHOST TOUR

Heading out onto the streets of Ybor City, you'll find a modern neighborhood buzzing with nightlife. And secrets. On the Ybor City Ghost Tour, the bowler-hatted tour guides share stories of the egotistical Cuban surgeon who left one wife for another and then another, and the mad son of a beloved doctor who is thought to be responsible for several murders. A highlight of the tour takes you into the home of the Cuban Club, where, with flashlight and ghost meter in hand, you'll creep into the dark theater in search of Ybor's ghosts. Whether you're there in search of orbs and blips or just history and a good time, this tour will take you into the basements and back rooms of some of Ybor's oldest places.

813-386-3905
yborghosttour.com

TRAVEL BACK IN TIME
AT THE HENRY B. PLANT MUSEUM

The minarets of the Henry B. Plant Museum and the University of Tampa look out across the Hillsborough River and over downtown Tampa like giant silver Hershey's Kisses. They're an iconic part of the Tampa skyline. Go inside the Plant Museum, which is just one wing of what was once the grand Tampa Bay Hotel, and you might feel transported to the past. This hotel, built by railroad magnate Henry Plant, was an extravagant destination for the wealthy starting in 1891. The museum was established in the 1930s and includes original furniture and decorations. Fun fact: the light bulbs inside burn at the same wattage they did in Plant's time, and they set a nice mood for exploring the hotel's ornate history.

401 W. Kennedy Blvd., Tampa
813-254-1891
plantmuseum.com

TIP

For most of the month of December, the Henry B. Plant Museum decks its halls in old Christmas style. The museum's Victorian Christmas Stroll includes trimmed trees, carolers, a display of antique toys, spiced cider, and Old Saint Nick.

GET THE STORIES
BEHIND ST. PETE'S STREET ART

Murals cover the walls of buildings, along alleys, even the street itself at an intersection. Each one tells a tale, and together they tell a story about street art in St. Pete. Join the Official Walking Mural Tour of St. Pete and experience a four-block, thirty-mural deep dive into the art, the artists, and how they came to make St. Pete beautiful. You'll learn the story behind the skateboarding granny on Central Avenue, the Twiggy mural on 1st Avenue North, and the mural painted on the street at Central Avenue and 5th Street. The walking tours take place every Saturday morning. If you want to see more of the murals around town, try the monthly bike tour. If you want to go it alone, the St. Petersburg Arts Alliance has a free, downloadable map and guide.

501 Central Ave., St. Petersburg
727-821-7391
floridacraftart.org/events

TIP

Celebrate St. Pete's mural tradition at the annual Shine Festival, which takes place in October.

stpeteartsalliance.org/shine-mural-festival

75

TIME TRAVEL FROM THE COMFORT OF HOME
WITH THE BURGERT BROTHERS PHOTOGRAPHIC COLLECTION

Here is the only entry in this book that doesn't actually require you to go somewhere. And while you can see some of the Burgert Brothers Photographic Collection at the John F. Germany Public Library in downtown Tampa, you can also see thousands of images from the comfort of your own computer screen. The Burgert family captured still images of life in Florida from the late 1800s until the 1960s. The library bought the collection in the '70s, saving it for the rest of us. After you've discovered their photographs, you can request one for yourself or order prints. The collection includes thousands of images that show stories of Tampa's past in vivid black and white.

900 N. Ashley Dr., Tampa
813-273-3652
hcplc.org/research/burgert

VISIT A CASTLE

IN ONA

Deep in the wilds of central Florida, down a private road and through a tall gate, you'll find a castle. Odd and charming, Solomon's Castle first began in 1972 when the late Howard Solomon started covering the outside of his home with offset printing plates from the county's newspaper. You'll hear all about this and about Solomon's work, from the famous reproductions to originals he's made from old beer cans, auto parts, and jack saws in this pun-filled tour. When that's done, stop by the Boat-in-the-Moat, run by the artist's daughter and son-in-law, for a drink and lunch at an equally odd and interesting spot. Tours run every day but Mondays, except in August and September, between 11 a.m. and 4 p.m.

4585 Solomon Rd., Ona
863-494-6077
solomonscastle.com

77

GO BACKSTAGE
AT THE TAMPA THEATRE

This ninety-minute Balcony-to-Backstage Tour takes you into the ornate 1920s movie palace, upstairs, and down into the basement, which happens to be under the sidewalk outside. Designed by famed theater architect John Eberson, the Tampa Theatre feels like a Spanish city at night, with stuffed doves, a peacock, and a mishmash style of décor one guide calls "Florida Mediterranean." The theater is a working one, showing six hundred films a year, including classics, family classics, and live performances. You can also appreciate the original décor, the elaborate restrooms, and the odd details here and there if you go to see a film. But take the tour, which takes place on select Tuesdays and Saturdays, for a fuller sense of the history and value of this place. And stay until the end for a performance on the Wurlitzer organ, which rises slowly out of the stage floor and is definitely a show all on its own.

711 N. Franklin St., Tampa
813-274-8981
tampatheatre.org

TIP

Get into the holiday spirit each December with a series of classic films that run weekends at the Tampa Theatre.

BE A DROP OF WATER
AT THE GLAZER CHILDREN'S MUSEUM

You could also be a vet. Or you could be a lighting tech, or a firefighter, or a dentist, or a meteorologist. This interactive downtown space offers kids a lot of chances to explore the world and the jobs they might someday have. The Glazer Children's Museum feels like it was created by master preschool teachers, with separate spaces for dress up, learning, and exploration. Several areas offer opportunities to learn more about a specific career and discipline, to build, to design, and to imagine. But kids can also pretend to be a drop of water and evaporate up into the third-floor ceiling in the vast and webbed climbing space. Then, they trickle back down, following the meandering path that water takes.

110 W. Gasparilla Plaza, Tampa
813-443-3861
glazermuseum.org

79

LOOK UP
AT THE HOTEL FLORIDAN

Outside this nineteen-story hotel, you'll see the giant red letters that have looked out over downtown Tampa for close to ninety years. Now, go inside. Again, look up. You'll find restored ceilings and glittering crystal chandeliers. The Floridan Palace, built in 1926, was Florida's first skyscraper, according to the hotel. The Floridan closed in 1989, but it got new life after restoration and reopening in 2012. You don't have to stay there, though, to get a glimpse of the past. Just stop in for a drink at the bar and, one last time, look up. The restored cypress ceilings are original to the building, as are the ornate ceilings inside the grand dining room with pink flowers nestled inside green leaves inside rows of golden octagons.

905 Florida Ave., Tampa
813-225-1700
floridanpalace.com

80

SEE A LIVING COLLECTION
BY FRANK LLOYD WRIGHT

Overlooking Lake Hollingsworth in Lakeland sits a collection of twelve buildings created by Frank Lloyd Wright. Wright's Child of the Sun was built at Florida Southern College largely by students. Today, stop by the Child of the Sun Visitor Center for a walking guide map, or stick around for the docent-led tour. You'll be able to see Wright's unmistakable fingerprint on your own in a few places, but the tour gets you into buildings still in use today. While on campus, take a few minutes to walk around the E. T. Roux Library, built mostly by female students and finished in 1945 while male students were fighting in World War II. And keep an eye out for lovely moments of old meeting new, like students chaining their bikes to Wright's perfectly planned structures.

111 Lake Hollingsworth Dr., Lakeland
863-680-4111
flsouthern.edu

TOUR A LANDMARK THAT'S COME BACK TO LIFE AT THE VINOY

You will not hear ghost stories while exploring this famous pink waterfront hotel in St. Petersburg. You will brush right up against the past, though. This confection of architecture has a fascinating history, with golden days in the 1920s, '30s, and '40s (including time as a military training center during World War II). By the '60s, it was pretty run down. The hotel closed in the early '70s and sat empty until 1992, when it reopened. It got a total makeover in 2008, and now it's restored to its original glam. You'll learn all of this and hear stories of the hotel that bring the past alive. Tours cost ten dollars and take place Wednesdays through Saturdays. Add in the three-course lunch in the classic dining room for twenty-seven dollars per person (including the tour), and you just might feel a bit of what it was like to stay here a long time ago.

501 5th Ave. Northeast, St. Petersburg
727-824-8033
marriott.com/hotel-info/tpasr-the-vinoy-renaissance-st-petersburg-resort-and-golf-club/history/czs6txk/tours.mi

82

GET TO KNOW THE PEOPLE OF TAMPA
AT THE TAMPA BAY HISTORY CENTER

Tampa Bay History Center sits on the Hillsborough River, with lovely views of downtown Tampa. Inside you'll find layers and levels of history to explore. Start on the second level to discover the first people of Tampa, including an immersive exhibit on Seminole chief Coacoochee that will have you feeling like you're in the middle of the swamp, hiding under the trees. On the third level, explore Florida agriculture and the people who've built their lives around it, and on the fourth level meet the conquistadors and pirates who sailed our waters. Visit around mealtime and you'll get to spend some time with another group of people—those who know about the waterfront version of one of Tampa's most famous eateries—Columbia Restaurant.

801 Old Water St., Tampa
813-228-0097
tampabayhistorycenter.org

SEE CHIHULY
IN ST. PETE

Even outside the Chihuly Collection at the Morean Arts Center, signs of the famous artist sprout in bright glass sculpture. Inside, find work from the Seattle artist known for elevating the craft of glass blowing into an art. And it's not all glass. Watch for vibrant Chihuly sketches that offer a look at where the now-famous work he creates begins. You will see the swirling curlicues and the flower-inspired shapes he's known for (think the Bellagio in Las Vegas), but the great diversity of his work shines here, too. Take time for the free docent tour, during which you'll hear the stories of what's behind the pieces and the man who made them. If you're feeling inspired afterward, head over to the Morean Arts Center Glass Studio and Hot Shop, where you can get a personal lesson is glass blowing.

720 Central Ave., St. Petersburg
727-822-7872
moreanartscenter.org/chihuly

SEE A LITTLE BIT OF CUBA
AT PARQUE AMIGOS DE JOSE MARTI

On a small square of land, behind a high fence, you can find a little bit of Cuba. A block or so away from Ybor City's 7th Avenue, Parque Amigos de Jose Marti is a tiny park that marks the site where a house once stood that often hosted Jose Marti, the Cuban revolutionary. The land itself is owned by Cuba, and the park is mostly locked up now, ironically, but still visible through the gate. While you're in Ybor soaking up the impact Cuban history had on Tampa history, stop by the Ybor City History Museum. Located in an old bakery, there's a restored home to explore and exhibits that tell the stories of other immigrants who came to Tampa to build new lives.

1303 E. 8th Ave., Tampa

LEAVE YOUR MARK
AT THE FLORIDA HOLOCAUST MUSEUM

You can tour the Florida Holocaust Museum on your own or join the free docent-led tour each Saturday at 1:30 p.m. Once you make it through the emotion-packed first floor, past small artifacts from the lives of victims of the Holocaust, past a boxcar that held Jews on their way to a concentration camp, and past a huge wall of photos, you'll reach a small room just for meditation and prayer. Here, take a moment and write a prayer of your own, fold it, and slip it into a crack in the museum's own replica of the Western Wall of the Temple Mount in Jerusalem.

55 5th St. South, St. Petersburg
727-820-0100
flholocaustmuseum.org

WATCH SAND BECOME SCULPTURE

You can leave your buckets and shovels at home for this trip to the beach. In Sarasota, the Siesta Key Crystal Classic is an international sand-sculpting festival featuring sand sculptors who have twenty-four hours to bring the sand to life with their work. Past sculptures include an intricate castle, a mermaid, and a life-sized car. The Crystal Classic takes place in November, and you do need tickets to get in to see the art and enjoy the festival. Around the same time, head over to Treasure Island for the Sanding Ovation Master's Cup for another set of sand marvels, which has featured an ice queen made of sand, a sandy Burt Reynolds, and giant hands steepled in prayer. This event, which is free, also includes a festival.

siestakeycrystalclassic.com
sandingovationsmasterscup.com

SEE THE NIGHT LIGHTS
AT THE TAMPA MUSEUM OF ART

There's a lot to see inside the Tampa Museum of Art, including an extensive twentieth-century photography collection. But if you stop by most nights as the sun sets, you'll see a work of art on the outside, too. Sky (Tampa) is a light show on the museum's aluminum-covered south side. Twelve thousand square feet of LED lights change every night in electric purples, blues, reds, pinks, and more. The installation, by artist Leo Villarreal, ripples, waves, and dances in vivid colors across the museum's exterior. Sky (Tampa) is a free show—just choose a spot in Curtis Hixon Park, or from the water, or across the water at the Plant Museum or the University of Tampa. Then sit back and marvel.

120 W. Gasparilla Plaza, Tampa
813-274-8130
tampamuseum.org

SEE THE WORLD'S BIGGEST TINIEST CIRCUS
AT THE RINGLING

Enclosed in glass, this huge model in the Circus Museum Tibbals Learning Center is a tiny testament to what it once took to run a circus. You'll see the dining tent, performers' quarters, wild animals, and performers behind the scenes, all frozen in miniature. Watch the light change as you slowly see behind the scenes at the circus, from tiny night to tiny day. The details of this forty-four-thousand-piece recreation of the circus days from 1919 to 1938 are small and still but totally alive. There's also an epic playground near the Banyan Cafe that's a great spot to sip a little wine and rest while the smallest people with you burn some energy. Wander down past Mabel's Rose Gardens toward Ca' d'Zan, the winter home of Mable and John Ringling, that sits like a Venetian palace on the water. You can tour inside and then walk or ride the trams over to see their impressive art collection. Make sure to stroll through the shady Dwarf Garden, full of small stone statues that give the space its name.

5401 Bay Shore Rd., Sarasota
941-359-5700
ringling.org

89

CHURN BUTTER, MAKE ROPE
AT CRACKER COUNTRY

Walk down the wooden ramp into Cracker Country, and with just a few steps, you'll get a glimpse of Florida's past. This small but packed area is a living history experience at the Florida State Fairgrounds. It has buildings from around Florida during the state's early days. Visit the Okahumpka train station, see homes and businesses, make rope or rag dolls, or just sit back and listen to good old-time music. Cracker Country was named for Florida's early settlers, known as Crackers, thanks to the sound their whips made in the air while rounding up cattle. It's open certain times during the year, including during the state fair and in December with a look at how Floridians once celebrated Christmas with Christmas in the Country.

4800 Highway 301 North, Tampa
813-621-7821
crackercountry.org

90

SHIFT INTO NEUTRAL
AT SPOOK HILL

Spook Hill has no real address, since it's, well, a hill. Small signs guide you to this old and popular spot in Lake Wales. Try starting from the hill's namesake elementary school nearby, then turn left. The large sign there will tell you the story of the legendary battle between the Indian chief and a terrorizing gator and the weird stuff that's happened there since. Roll up to the white line in the road, flip your car into neutral, and watch as you roll slightly up hill. That's pretty much it. Some people love it. Some aren't that impressed. But you should try it for yourself because, as one local put it, "At least it's free."

Wales Dr. and J.A. Wiltshire, Lake Wales
lakewaleschamber.com/spook-hill

WALK THROUGH THE PAST

AT HERITAGE VILLAGE

Nestled under towering palmettos and pines in a large park in Largo, Heritage Village stretches out like an old town just might, with a grocery store, a mechanic shop, a post office, a church, a school, and a few homes. Inside those buildings, women sew, men carve, and people wash clothes and cook the old-fashioned way. The twenty-one-acre village has several annual events, including a Country Jubilee and Holidays at the Village. Heritage Village is open year round, and admission is free. Check out the map online before you go, and make sure to stop by the EnterAction Stations, which offer a do-it-yourself adventure for young pioneers as they get a glimpse of life in the past.

11909 125th St., Largo
727-582-2123
pinellascounty.org/heritage

HEAR THE BELLS
AT BOK TOWER GARDENS

Recordings of the bells' songs play every half hour from this 205-foot Gothic tower surrounded by a small pool of water and twisting black iron gates in Lake Wales. Bok Tower was built in 1929 by Edward Bok, who became editor of the *Ladies' Home Journal*. The Dutch immigrant built the fairy-tale tower as a gift to his new country, and it holds sixty carillon bells that ring and sing with live concerts during the weekends through the fall and spring. Bok Tower sits on Iron Mountain, the highest spot in peninsular Florida, and it is surrounded by lovely gardens, mulched paths, and some of nature's own music, too. While at Bok Tower, visit nearby Pinewood Estates, a 1930s home that you can tour throughout the year.

1151 Tower Blvd., Lake Wales
863-676-1408
boktowergardens.org

GET LOST WITH DALI

This waterfront museum home of avant-garde artist Salvador Dali is an adventure to explore, just like Dali's art itself. From the outside, the windows of the Dali Museum bubble and pour out of the stately, modernist cube. Inside, a long staircase spirals up, mirroring the inside of a shell. Get some headphones for the free audio tour and listen in as the life and work of this Spanish surrealist unfold from room to room. While there, stop by the waterfront Avant-gardens, where you can get lost in the labyrinth, explore the grotto, and, before you leave, take off your paper entry band, make a wish, and tie it to one of the hundreds already draping down from The Wish Tree.

One Dali Blvd., St. Petersburg
727-823-3767
thedali.org

MAR CALIFORNIA
4U46468
CALIFORNIA
4U46468
COMMERCIAL
CA-80767
PENNSYLVANIA
PENNSYLVANIA
F26 720
BICENTENNIAL STATE 76
1980
SUMMIT OF
PIKES PEAK
ALT. 14,110 FEET
BERMUDA

SHOPPING AND FASHION

HUNT FOR ANTIQUES
IN PLANT CITY

Plant City is known as the home of the Florida Strawberry Festival, but if you've been downtown, you'll know it's also the home of great antique shopping. Around the main square downtown, store after store of antiques fan out. Some shops only sell rare and expensive treasures, but most feature a mix of antiques, repurposed and repainted furniture, odd treasures, and new finds. Explore the area in search of vintage dresses, old signs, funky furniture, costume jewelry, creepy baby dolls, and new ways to use old things. Try State Theatre, an old movie house that now sells interesting antiques, or Chic Antiques, which sells vintage finds with modern touches. From either place, head out the door and start walking for more.

plantcity.org

95

FIND IT, WHATEVER IT IS,
AT THE BIG TOP FLEA MARKET

Bingo supplies. Boiled peanuts. Cowboy boots. Beer. Books. Body jewelry. Underwear. Smokes. Swords. Silk flowers. Vacuum bags. Cornhole boards. Knives. Baseball cards. Birds. Bunnies. Fudge. Haircuts. Instant snow. Bamboo wind chimes. Bonsai trees. Dishes. Keyboards. Vinyl. Kayaks. The Big Top Flea Market, open Saturdays and Sundays, is a carnival of stuff with fourteen wings of shopping, including a whopping 1,200 booths on thirty-six acres. Luckily, there's also food and drinks, which you'll need, especially if you forget to write down where you came in and get lost for a while. Not that that has actually happened to anyone. . . . Consider downloading a map before you venture out. The market also recommends wearing comfortable shoes. And maybe bring your phone charger. If you forget it, though, you can easily buy one here.

9250 E. Fowler Ave., Tampa
813-986-4004
bigtopfleamarket.com

chiller's
design salvage

SALVAGE SOMETHING
FROM THE PAST AT SCHILLER'S

Before you even set foot into Schiller's Architectural and Design Salvage in Tampa, there's shopping to do. Sift (and lift) through piles of old letters, wood, windows, and doors outside. Once you're inside, explore the marvelous maze of salvaged stuff—ornate doors and windows, soft red movie theater seats, old safe deposit boxes, rescued and reclaimed wood, stained glass windows, crystal door knobs, antique light fixtures, blueprints, maps, and more. You can find special pieces of Florida history here, too, including reliefs from the Tampa Theatre, aisles of pieces from the Belleview Biltmore Resort and Spa, and original pine floors from the Tampa Bay Hotel. Make sure you look up high and down low during your visit. The treasures are everywhere.

1002 N. Rome Ave., Tampa
813-443-4641
schillersalvage.com

97

DIG FOR BEACH TREASURES

AT THE SAND DOLLAR ON AMI

If you need a break from the shell hunting or the soft sand or the blue water or the perfect sunsets on Anna Maria Island, check out the Sand Dollar Gift Shop. This spot, at one end of the Holmes Beach Plaza, is packed with treasures to bring home from the beach, including polished shells, decorative sand, candles, drapey beach dresses, trendy sandals, dangly earrings, wreaths, rugs, Anna Maria Island maps, and memorabilia. It's a great way to bring a bit of the beach home. After you shop here, check out other stores in the plaza and nearby for more shop-able island charm. You probably need more mermaid décor, anyway.

5302 Marina Dr., Holmes Beach
941-778-2024

WINDOW SHOP AND PEOPLE WATCH
AT ST. ARMANDS CIRCLE

John Ringling's vision of a shopping and living area on St. Armands Key first began in 1926. Now, you'll find an interesting mix of fashion, jewelry, salons, restaurants, and galleries. Give yourself some time to explore St. Armands, which literally is a circle surrounding a park, with streets shooting out in four directions. Those streets are also filled with shops, restaurants, and places to explore. Take note of the stately statues sprinkled around the area, including Dionysus, a bust of Ringling himself, and a few appearances by Venus. The people watching at St. Armands is just as good as the shopping, by the way. From flip-flopped vacationers to puppy-stroller-pushing locals, it's all a circus for the eyes.

visitsarasota.com/lido-key-st-armands

99

STROLL CENTRAL AVENUE
IN ST. PETE

You'll find local breweries and boutiques, food and furniture, antiques and art, and so much more along Central Avenue in St. Petersburg. This street, tucked between 1st Avenue North and 1st Avenue South, is packed with places to shop and stop for a break. Central encompasses two distinct districts: Central Arts District, from the three hundred to seven hundred blocks, and the Grand Central District, from 16th to 31st streets. Check out First Friday St. Pete every first Friday of the month, with food, music, and artisans on Central between 2nd and 3rd streets. Plus, you can do your homework before you hit the road with an interactive map that includes places you can find parking so you can get to strolling.

Central Avenue, between 1st Ave. North and 1st Ave. South
St. Petersburg
discoverdowntown.com

100

MARK YOUR CALENDAR FOR THE TREASURE HUNTING
AT BROCANTE VINTAGE MARKET

One weekend each month, Brocante Vintage Market opens its doors to 1,500 square feet of treasures. The line starts early, but it's well worth the wait to see the furniture, clothes, art, books, and more that are themselves arranged like works of art from floor to ceiling. You'll see black-and-white family portraits; ornate, repainted frames; upcycled pieces; dishes; jewelry; silver; china; and dogs. Many dogs. They're not for sale, but you can bring yours with you if, say, he or she enjoys a good vintage market (although remember, it does get crowded, so maybe save shopping with your pup for the slightly less crazy Sunday markets). If you're up early and shopping, stop by the weekly Saturday Morning Market in St. Pete, which runs October through May, and the St. Pete Indie Market, which runs at the same time.

2200 2nd Ave. South, St. Petersburg
brocantemarket.com
saturdaymorningmarket.com
stpeteindiemarket.com

SUGGESTED ITINERARIES

DATE NIGHTS

HISTORY SEEKERS AND CULTURE BUFFS

BEACHGOERS

FANS

MOVERS

EATERS AND DRINKERS

WITH THE KIDDOS

SHOPPERS AND BROWSERS

MUSIC LOVERS

CLASSIC FLORIDA

SEASONAL ACTIVITIES

WINTER

SPRING

SUMMER

FALL

INDEX